For Carolyn

FOOD
& FEAST
IN MEDIEVAL
ENGLAND

PETER HAMMOND

SUTTON PUBLISHING

This book was first published in 1993 by
Sutton Publishing Limited · Phoenix Mill
Thrupp · Stroud · Gloucestershire · GL5 2BU

This revised paperback edition first published in 2005

British Library Cataloguing in Publication Data
A catalogue record for this book is available from the British
Library.

ISBN 0 7509 3773 4

Typeset in 11/13.5pt Photina.
Typesetting and origination by
Sutton Publishing Limited.
Printed and bound in Great Britain by
J.H. Haynes & Co. Ltd, Sparkford.

CONTENTS

LIST OF ILLUSTRATIONS

PREFACE

Food is a perennially interesting subject and the food of
the Middle Ages has the added attraction of being less
known than food of the more recent past. In many
ways the food (and the way it was eaten) was very different,
in others it is very similar to our own. It is hoped that this
book will serve as an introduction to this very interesting
subject.

The book will deal with the food eaten, who ate what, the
manners of those that ate it and whether or not it would
have nourished (or poisoned) them. The period covered is
from about 1250 to about 1550. Things changed in such a
long period but surprisingly little in many ways. Changes
will be pointed out where relevant. There is a bias towards
the fifteenth century since many good sources date from
that time. Cooking is not covered at all, mainly because I
am not a cook in any sense, nor is household organization
dealt with in any great detail.

It only remains for me to thank those who have helped me,
their names will be found in the references but I want to
mention particularly Dave Scuffam for his usual excellent
drawings, Tony Dove for advice on medieval eating
implements, and above all my wife Carolyn for, as usual, her
indispensable help in reading the text and for helping in other

innumerable ways. To her this book is dedicated with apologies for the lack of chocolate.

This edition contains an Afterword, (pp. 148–155), taking into account some of the major new work published since the book was first written.

PWH

ONE

WHERE FOOD CAME FROM

Food in the Middle Ages was not so very different from food today. People ate much the same things: meat, such as beef, pork and lamb (or mutton); fruit and vegetables; and grain prepared in various ways, such as bread and ale. Those who could afford it drank wine. Their diet was a far from restricted one, and the variety of foodstuffs available to those with the means to buy was very wide. Much food was imported through such ports as London, Southampton and Bristol, some was brought considerable distances. Spices were easily available, some of them coming from the Far East, and dried fruit (such as 'raisins of Corinth') was imported from the eastern Mediterranean. Sweet wines came from the same area and ordinary wines from all the wine-growing regions of Europe. Exotic fruits, such as oranges, lemons and pomegranates, were imported, particularly in the fifteenth century and later. Fish came from as far afield as Iceland, much of it salted but some of it fresh. This range of food was supported by a sophisticated internal distribution network. Fresh sea fish, for example, were easily bought in such inland towns as Coventry. The preparation of the food was rather different from modern methods, a spicier flavour was preferred than is generally thought desirable today in England, and dishes were frequently coloured. A considerable amount of broth and soup-like dishes and far more fish than today, much of it salted, were eaten on the many fast days when other animal flesh was forbidden. This chapter describes where the food came from, beginning with grain of various kinds, since the staple food of all classes was bread and ale (brewed from barley or other grain).

The main crops planted were grain of several kinds, such as wheat, rye, barley and oats. Some peas and beans were also grown. In the south the main crop grown on the demesne land (that is, estate land owned by the lord of the manor), was usually wheat. This was the most commercially valuable crop since wheaten bread was more desirable than any other kind. In the fifteenth century this trend changed to a more general concentration on barley and oats, since these gave higher yields. Much barley was grown, sometimes more than wheat, because it was valuable as a source of ale as well as bread. Most of the oats were grown in northern England, where the climate was not so well suited to wheat and barley. Oats were needed throughout the country to feed horses. The proportion of different grains grown varied widely, depending on period, soil and climate. In the first quarter of the fourteenth century, Bolton Priory produced about 80 per cent oats, with about 12 per cent wheat and the rest consisting of rye, barley and beans; in Cuxham, Oxfordshire, about 50 per cent wheat was sown in the autumn and (from the middle of the fourteenth century) about 50 per cent oats in the spring. In the fifteenth century (c. 1430) in Norfolk, 13 per cent wheat was being grown at one manor, Easton Bavents, with 17 per cent rye, 59 per cent barley and the rest peas.[1] It was wise to grow a fairly wide variety of crops to spread the risk of failure. Most of the bread eaten by peasants was probably made from rye, and it seems likely that this was the main crop grown by them for much of the Middle Ages. It is much the hardiest grain and grows in most soils.[2]

Mixed seed was also sown, for example dredge (or drage: barley and oats) and berevechicorn (dredge and vetch) which were used as fodder. Vetch, sown alone, was also used as fodder, but both this and berevechicorn would have been used for human consumption in times of famine. Other mixed crops included maslin (rye and wheat), pulse (beans and peas) and the delightfully named bollymong (or bullymong: oats, peas and vetches or buckwheat). The problem with sowing mixed seed was that they tended to ripen at different times. It has been suggested that for this reason they were rarely sown together; it is possible, however, that these mixtures were frequently sown (it would have been much simpler) and that they were then harvested, in the case of maslin, for example, just after the rye ripened and just before the wheat did so. There seem to have been no fixed proportions of the components of these mixtures.[3] For each seed type, more than one strain existed, and the appropiate type was sown according to the lightness or heaviness of the soil in the area. There were different varieties of peas and beans too. The grey bean, for example, a type of broad bean, was chiefly grown as fodder, but was also eaten by the very poorest people.

All of these seeds were planted at different times of the year. Wheat and rye were sown after the autumn ploughing, between Michaelmas and Christmas, and were known as the winter seed. The rest, sown in the early spring, were the Lenten seed (Lent was loosely spoken of as the period between Christmas and Easter). All of them matured at about the same time in August and September. This arrangement helped to spread the load of heavy work (apart from the harvest). The agricultural system employed usually involved part of the land lying fallow for a year between crops to help the soil recover its fertility. This was not a very efficient way of cultivation so yields were less than they could have been. Crop rotation was also not a very effective means of improving the yield and the lack of variety in the crops grown would not have helped either. Fertility could be improved by keeping cattle and sheep on fields that were fallow or which had just been cropped, thus manuring them. The Lord of the manor frequently tried to make his tenants fold their animals, particularly sheep, on the demesne land rather than on their own land, thus improving his soil at the tenants' expense. Occasionally marl (a natural fertilizer made of clay and limestone) was spread on the fields, although it was neither easy to obtain nor to transport. Sand or seaweed were used where available. Not all lords were as enlightened as the first Lord Berkeley who encouraged his tenants to use the earth from the green highways of the manors. More usually, fertilizer was made by putting the straw from the previous year's harvest (if this was not being used to supplement the cattle's diet) in the cowsheds and stables over the winter. Landowners were well aware of the need to manure the land, to plough in the stubble, if possible, and the use of 'doung'. They were also well aware of the need to prevent the seed from being eaten before it germinated, and used primitive pesticides such as the juice of wild cucumber or wild leek. These would probably have made the seed unpalatable to mice and birds too. They also used oil dregs or soot against snails.[4]

Attempts have been made to estimate the yield of corn obtained. Figures are inevitably based on the harvests of the lord's fields since no data exist for those of the peasants. Since the ability of the latter to manure the land was not as great as that of the lord, peasants' yields would have been considerably lower. Walter of Henley, in about 1280, thought that just over seven bushels of wheat had to be harvested from every acre in order to make a profit, unless the price of wheat was particularly high. This was based on sowing about two (or slightly more) bushels of wheat and rye to the acre. Oats and barley were sown at about the same rate in the Middle Ages but at a slightly higher rate in the sixteenth century. After a poor harvest, less seed corn would be saved and less could be sown the following year. There was always a fine line between having only enough to eat and producing sufficient to sow the following year. If there was not enough the poor harvest tended to be repeated. The yield from various manors throughout England is known and, as might be expected, varied from more than Walter of Henley's theoretical figure to considerably less. The yield of wheat in the north, where conditions were not really suitable, tended to be very low, while that of oats was good. Peasants probably sowed only a little pure wheat, concentrating more on mixtures, such as maslin and drage, as well as pure oats, barley and rye, and possibly peas and beans. Considering only wheat, barley and rye to simplify the calculations, it has been shown that from 20 acres (about the usual holding), a peasant probably obtained approximately 48 bushels of wheat, 66 bushels of barley and 39 bushels of oats. This was after the allowance for the following year's seed had been deducted and ignoring the tithe (a proportion of the harvest paid to the Church) which was taken before the crops were reaped. This compares with a yield of some 20 bushels to the acre of wheat, 32 of barley and 40 of oats and beans on better-fertilized land in the sixteenth century.[5]

Much of the grain grown was eaten or set aside for sowing the following year. However some of it, mostly the barley, was used to make ale, employing a technique similar to that used today. First the barley was malted (that is it was allowed to germinate), heated to stop growth and then roasted. By this process all the starch in the grain was converted to soluble starch and a pleasant flavour given to the product. After this the rootlets were removed, and the malted barley crushed and then heated with water. This extracted the soluble starches which were converted by enzymes to soluble sugars. Next the mixture was cooled and yeast added, which caused fermentation into ale. By tradition only barley, water and yeast were allowed to be used in this process. The yeast was obtained from the previous brewing or from other brewers (it multiplies itself in the fermenting liquid). It was sometimes sold, particularly to bakers who also needed it, and regulations were laid down that the price should not be excessive since it was an essential commodity. It was decided in Norwich in 1468 that, for a quantity sufficient to make one quarter of malt (that is eight bushels, or about 400 lb) into ale, a brewer should not charge more than a farthing. The water was obtained from the nearest river or other usable source. It was necessary to have fairly pure water, and in London the brewers frequently used the various conduits bringing in drinking water, much to the annoyance of the other users. Thus in 1345 they were forbidden to use the water from the conduit in the Chepe because it was meant for 'rich and middling persons' to use 'for preparing their food'. This was repeated in other towns, for example Coventry in the middle of the sixteenth century.[6] As the fifteenth century progressed, beer (that is ale brewed with hops) became more and more common, despite attempts to suppress it on the grounds that hops adulterated the ale (see Chapter 4). Ale itself had long been adulterated in private brewing by the addition of spices or herbs, but using hops allowed the product to be kept longer: hops contain natural preservatives. Ale lacking hops goes off very quickly, so it was necessary to brew frequently in the Middle Ages.

Much of the brewing was carried out by women, either for consumption in the home or for sale in alehouses. This seems to have ceased with the introduction of hops, perhaps because using hops made the process too technically complicated for the small brewer.[7] Very large amounts of ale were drunk in the Middle Ages. It was the common drink of all classes and many hundreds of gallons were used by a large household. In the case of the household of Humphrey Stafford, Duke of Buckingham, during 1452–3 over forty thousand gallons were consumed in one year. The monks of Westminster used about eighty thousand gallons in a year, so correspondingly large areas were needed to carry out the brewing. The malt-house at Fountains Abbey, Yorkshire, for example, has a steeping vessel about 18 feet in diameter (in a building nearly 60 feet square) that would have been capable of dealing with 20 quarters of barley every 10 to 12 days, making at least 60 barrels (each holding about 36 gallons) of very strong ale. Ale was brewed commercially to two different strengths, while home-brewed ale could be made to any desired strength and was supposed to be sold at a set price depending on the cost of barley (see Chapter 2).[8]

Fruit and vegetables were also grown. These were not produced on a large scale as most of the crop was eaten by those who grew it, but there was a certain amount of market gardening (see Chapter 3). Apples and pears were the major crop, of which several varieties were available. One of the earliest recorded types of apple was the Pearmain, and a very large variety, the Costard, was popular. Others included Pippins, and a particular variety, such as the Blanderelle, was sometimes specified as being bought or needed for a particular recipe. The most popular pear was the large and very hard 'Warden'. It cost more than ordinary types (frequently more than any variety of apple) and was very often used in cooking. Some cherries were grown for sale as well as for home eating, as were strawberries, although most of the records for the latter are from the sixteenth century. Strawberries were not easy to grow commercially. Vegetables too were chiefly grown for home use, but some were sold, particularly in towns (see Chapter 3).[9]

The three main large food animals were cows, sheep and pigs. Kids were eaten also, chiefly in the early part of the period, in the thirteenth century. They are rarely mentioned in accounts of the fourteenth and fifteenth centuries and never in such numbers as on the Continent. Pigs were kept in far larger numbers (if not very large, an average of three per household on the estates of the Bishop of Worcester in the mid-fourteenth century) since they provided much meat and were relatively easy to fatten, feeding on what they could pick up from village waste and fallows. When the land available for them to roam on was large, they were expected to be self-supporting for nine months of the year. Sometimes after Christmas they were given extra food. The number of cows kept by each peasant was nearly always fewer than that of pigs, frequently not more than one or two per holding. For example, a group of fairly well-off villeins in Cuxham, Oxfordshire, in the early fourteenth century had only one each. The number of cattle kept was restricted in some villages, to avoid running the risk of over-grazing the meadows. Only those actually kept on a villager's own tenement were allowed onto the common land to graze. The cattle were turned onto the fallow field as soon as the hay harvest was finished, then back onto the meadow land after the hay had been cut at Lammas (1 August) until the grass began to grow again. Candlemas (2 February) was the traditional day to remove the cattle from the hay meadows, and from the field that was to be ploughed and sown that spring.[10] The number of cattle would also have been restricted by the inability to overwinter very many because of the lack of feed: the amount of hay obtained from the few hay meadows available was small.

The lord of the manor would always have had more cows than the villagers, and some manors bred cows in large numbers for town markets (see Chapter 3). The cow was important as a source of milk, butter and cheese, and of meat when slaughtered. Sheep meat in the form of mutton was eaten, but was not as popular as beef. By the fifteenth century more lamb than mutton was eaten (in the form of roast meat). Sheep, too, were an important source of milk and cheese, and there were many more sheep than cows since they were also kept for their wool. It has been estimated that in England in the fourteenth century there were at least 8 million sheep (that was the number of fleeces exported during the reign of Edward III). Some flocks, in the north of England particularly, numbered tens of thousands. Six to ten ewes were usually expected to give about as much milk as one cow (or ¼ gallon of butter and 7 lb of cheese). Sheep milking usually stopped on about Lammas Day (12 August), since if continued for longer there was a risk of weakening the sheep so much that they would not survive the winter. Most of the cow's milk, too, was obtained in the summer because of the scarcity of winter feed. It was usually estimated that four-fifths of a cow's annual milk yield was obtained during the twenty-four weeks from the middle of April to Michaelmas (29 September). Winter milk usually fetched three times the summer price, and the price obtained for milk over an eight-week period in winter was usually reckoned to be worth more than a calf. Calves were usually arranged to be born in the autumn. The total annual milk yield per cow in the fourteenth century has been calculated as 120–150 gallons, which is less than a sixth of that expected from a modern animal. Nor was the weight of meat obtained from cows and sheep as great as today. This was partly owing to poor feeding, but also to the lack of selective breeding. Approximate dead weight figures of 320 lb for a cow and 28 lb for a sheep have been calculated for the year 1500. The weight for a sheep had risen to about 45 lb by 1612. The average now is now about 60 lb for a sheep and 490 lb for a cow.[11]

As already mentioned, cheese, much of it from skim milk, and butter were made from both cows and sheep. The butter milk and whey were also used as drink (or more rarely to feed to pigs). The curds were used in cooking or drunk. Milk was rarely drunk by the rich, but was more often used in cooking. The 'white meats', milk, and milk products were thought of sometimes as the food of the poor, but this attitude overlooked the very large quatities of them all used in cooking.[12]

Many chickens were kept and geese too. The number of geese kept in a village sometimes required a gooseherd to look after them. The lord also sometimes had herds of his own, bought to be fattened on a paste made with milk and a flour of wheat and oats until they were ready to be eaten. The peasant probably always kept hens and was sometimes expected to produce eggs for the lord at given seasons, such as Christmas. Eggs were sometimes provided for the lord from his demesne manors (17,000 from two manors in the case of Lord Berkeley in the fourteenth century, together with 1,008 pigeons, several hundred chickens and other birds). Walter of Henley at the end of the thirteenth century thought that a hen should lay 180 eggs in a year, the author of *Husbandry* (of the same date) suggested more realistically that 115 eggs and seven chicks was the number to expect. The geese would lay eggs too and both birds would be used for meat.[13]

Sugar and spices played an important part in food in the Middle Ages, as did honey, which was used extensively in cooking for sweetening, although sugar was known and was used more and more as the Middle Ages progressed. Honey was also used in making mead and 'metheglin' (spiced mead). Large amounts were imported all around the country, although as early as the reign of Henry II sugar also was being imported to serve the purpose of sweetening. At this date sugar was very expensive, but by 1264 the price had dropped to 2s. /lb (10p) and by 1334 it could be bought for 7d. (3p). Prices remained very similar to this until well into the sixteenth century, although the actual figure depended on the degree of refinement. Very large amounts of sugar were used by the royal household before the end of the thirteenth century (6,258 lb in 1288), and from then on increasing amounts were imported. One ship alone, which entered Bristol from Lisbon in 1480, carried nearly 10 tons.[14] Sugar was imported from all over the Mediterranean, as were the luxuries that an increasing demand for sweet things encouraged. These included 'sugre candi' brought into London in 1421 from Italy, 'citronade' (candied lemon or orange peel) and large quantities of 'succade' (fruit preserved in sugar syrup), the latter two both brought on one of the Venetian state galleys in 1481. Considerable amounts of treacle, as well as violet and rose sugar, were brought in too. The sugars were more expensive than regular sugar and were partly used as medicine. Ordinary sugar was available in varying degrees of fineness, although most of it came in the form of 'loaves', which varied in size from about 1 lb to about 20 lb.[15]

Sugar was classed as a spice in the Middle Ages, and all of the things now thought of as spices were imported with it. Items such as ginger (in various grades), mace, cloves, cumin, cardamom, nutmegs, saffron, cinnamon, as well as more exotic spices including galingale, zedoary (both roots resembling ginger), cubebs (resembling pepper) and 'grains of paradise' (the seeds of a West African plant resembling ginger), were brought in regularly in moderate quantities. Pepper came in much larger amounts. The same ship that imported the succade also carried over 2 tons of pepper.[16] Most of the spices came from the East, on the old spice route, and were consequently expensive. Even pepper, the most common spice but not the cheapest, sold at about 1s./lb (5p) throughout the Middle Ages. The most expensive spice, and for some reason much more so after the Great Plague, was saffron (partly home grown), which, after 1349, sold at over 14s./lb (70p). The other spices were generally rather more expensive than pepper at about 2s. to 4s. (10p to 20p) /lb, but prices varied very widely depending on the season and other variables. One spice not imported was the native mustard. This was used in large amounts and could be bought for a farthing a pound, or less.[17]

The same ships that carried spices also tended to carry fruit, such as oranges, of which a surprising number were brought to England. These were frequently imported in the tens of thousands per ship, and occasionally as many as a hundred thousand (in March 1480). These oranges were probably always a bitter variety. For customs purposes they were declared at about ten for 1d. Other exotic fruit, such as pomegranates and lemons, were also imported, together with the common apple, and dried fruit such as figs, dates and very large amounts of raisins (frequently 'raisins of Corinth'). Nuts, such as walnuts and filberts, were brought too, although the latter were also grown in England. Very large quantities of almonds were imported since they were used very extensively in the cooking of the period (see Chapter 6). The royal household alone used over 48,000 lb in the two years of 1286 and 1287. Many of the nuts and apples came from France. Rice was imported from Spain and Italy. In the early fifteenth century it cost 1d./lb, rising later that century to 2d. or 3d. The same royal household with an appetite for almonds used nearly 10,000 lb of rice in the two years 1286 and 1287.[18]

Much wine was drunk in England in the Middle Ages. A certain amount was produced in England, although by the reign of Henry III the output was decreasing from its peak, possibly because of the new ease with which it could be imported from Gascony. Some wine was still produced in the reign of Henry VIII. Most of this was produced on the royal estates or those of the Church, and as far north as Leicestershire and Norfolk, although some small estates also produced limited amounts. It appears to have been mostly white wine, and was probably not of very good quality (although William of Malmesbury said in the mid-twelfth century that much excellent wine was produced in England), and in some years the grapes did not ripen sufficiently to make anything but 'verjuice' (squeezed and fermented sour juice). Most of the produce of English vineyards in the Middle Ages seems to have been verjuice. In 1289 seven pipes (a pipe was 126 gallons) of white wine and nearly one of verjuice were produced from the episcopal vineyard at Ledbury, owned by Richard de Swinfield, Bishop of Hereford. Swinfield seems to have expected to drink his own wine for at least part of the time. The seven pipes of wine were apparently valued at about half the price of the same quantity of imported wine bought in Bristol. By far the greatest volume of wine drunk in England was imported, however.[19]

Wine was imported through all the ports in England, although the greatest quantity came through the port of London. Wine came from the whole of France, including Burgundy, Normandy, Poitou, Anjou and, above all, Gascony. The amount imported varied according to the state of the economy and the quantity of the vintage. In the early fourteenth century about 20,000 tuns (casks) of wine were imported from Gascony alone, but this declined considerably after the start of the Hundred Years War. Then, even in a particularly good year in the fifteenth century, for example in 1414–15, the total was only 18,000 tuns (still over 4½ million gallons). Less still was imported later that century, until it rose again in the reign of Henry VII. In 1559–60, during Elizabeth I's reign, the total briefly reached 100,000 tuns.[20] These quantities were easily absorbed. In 1243, for example, Henry III alone bought no less than 1,445 casks of French (probably Gascon) wine at a cost of £2,310 2s. 8d. If a cask was equal to the standard English tun of 252 wine gallons, this was over 350,000 wine gallons. The wines were of mixed quality: 999 of the casks were of the top quality at

37s. a cask; 404 casks were of low quality at 20s. per cask. This bought wine was in addition to the wine obtained by the royal household as 'prisage': the two casks seized by the royal butler or his deputies from every cargo (sometimes sold by the king to raise money) and was the only wine bought by the royal household from London and Sandwich.[21] The returns of the right of prisage give some idea of the amount of wine that the king obtained by this means and also the amount of wine imported. In 1280, for example, the king obtained 238 casks of wine from London alone, representing at least 119 cargoes (the customs returns may not be complete). Prisage at some ports was sometimes granted to a debtor or favourite of the king. For example, the Archbishop of York had the prisage of wine at Hull for many years.

The amount of wine needed on some occasions was great. In 1316 Edward II ordered 2,600 tuns (probably more than 650,000 wine gallons) of wine for the supply of the army in his Scottish campaign (later topped up with another 1,400 casks). Edward III only needed 300 tuns of wine for his expedition in 1327, but in 1543 no less than sixteen ships were required to carry the wine for the annual provision of the household of Henry VIII. King Henry did not get this wine as the ships were captured by the Scots. Something similar seems to have happened to the wine for his troops in France in 1544, since it was reported that the soldiers remained inactive for some time due to a lack of supplies, having to go for several days without wine – apparently a great privation. At the Field of the Cloth of Gold, Henry himself is said to have had 3,000 butts of wine with him. That these considerable quantities of wine could be consumed quite easily is shown by allocating the apparently normal ration in the fourteenth century of 1 quart a day per head to the garrison of one of the royal castles, for example Dover. This garrison consisted of a thousand men when the castle was on a war footing. In forty days they would consume 10,000 gallons of wine, that is 40 tuns. Large amounts of wine were also consumed at coronations. For example, Edward II ordered 1,000 casks of good Gascon wine for his coronation, although Richard III seems to have had only just over 10 tuns.[22]

The import of wine was complicated in various ways by laws and regulations. When a cargo of wine arrived in port it was first visited by the king's butler or, more likely, his representative in that port who took the two casks due to his royal master as prisage (or allowed the merchant to pay him the value of two casks). He also bought any wine that the king needed. Prisage was only paid by English natives. Foreigners paid 'butlerage', which was a tax of 2s. per cask of wine imported. This rate was agreed between Edward I and the vintners of Gascony in 1302. When allowing for the value of two casks of wine, it meant that the natives and foreigners paid approximately the same amount. The rate of butlerage remained unchanged throughout the fourteenth, fifteenth and sixteenth centuries. This meant that, as the value of a cask of wine rose, natives paid more tax than foreign merchants. The native merchants tried to obtain exemptions of various kinds, either for smaller ships, for which it was proportionately a heavier tax, or for various ports. Freemen of the city of London obtained exemption, as did the Cinque ports. In the sixteenth century the prisage was finally set at a fixed rate per tun.

Another tax paid by wine importers, native and foreign alike, was 'tunnage'. This was a sum per tun of wine, the amount varying with the type of wine (usually more on sweet wine), and was granted to the monarch by Parliament for variable periods, sometimes for life. After this the ship owner was allowed to land the wine, but in London only at the Vintry, above London Bridge, and with the help of wine drawers whose charges were laid down and without whom no wine was supposed to be landed. No wine was allowed to be sold from the ship and forestalling, that is selling wine before it could reach the open market, was also strictly forbidden (see Chapter 2). Wine was not supposed to be moved unless each master wine drawer had twelve associates with him, 'instructed and skilled in the business'.[23] The wine was stored in warehouses allocated for this purpose (bonded warehouses in a sense), since no wine could legally be sold from them until every barrel had been gauged (that is the contents measured by calculation of the dimensions). After this, the cost of the gauging as well as the customs duties having been paid, the merchant was free to sell his wine, but only through wine brokers. These brokers were members of the Vintners' Guild which had a monopoly of the retail trade in Gascon wine in London, and their scale of charges was laid down too. Everyone was free to buy wholesale from the shippers, from one or two barrels each autumn and spring by the tavern keepers to large amounts by the vintners of the cities.[24]

Another source of food was wild fruit and nuts, collected from nearby woods and lands. This was allowed by the lord who owned these areas, unlike the gathering of wood which was strictly controlled. How much food was found in this way must have been very variable, depending on, for example, the weather and the area. In the area surrounding the cultivated land there must have been a great deal of wildlife including rabbits, hares and pheasants. Small birds could be trapped by netting or perhaps limed (caught using bird lime) and used for the pot. This hunting and gathering was complicated by the laws which never made it easy for peasants to hunt, even if they were not actually forbidden. Poaching rabbits, for example, was a fairly frequent offence (judging by the records of the manorial courts), and most lords, who ate them in large numbers themselves, tried to stop it. Rabbits were a nuisance in some parts of the country, so catching them may have been regarded partly as revenge for ruining the peasants' crops. In 1340 the men of Ovingdean, Sussex, complained that in their manor there were 100 acres of arable land where crops had been destroyed by the rabbits of their lord, Earl Warenne. In the fourteenth century an *inquisition post mortem* noted that a holding in Sussex was of low value because rabbits had started to burrow there.[25]

Another source of food for the lord were doves. These were bred in dovecotes, some of which were very large and held hundreds of pairs of birds. Quite large numbers, therefore, were eaten. The manor of Cuxham, Oxfordshire, produced up to 1,500 young doves each year until *c.* 1335, when the numbers appear to have dropped drastically. The dove was considered to be a great delicacy and peasants were forbidden to eat it, in practice, however, they did. Doves must have been relatively easy to trap, particularly when they came down in large numbers to eat the crops grown by the peasant. They were a particularly disliked example of the lord's authority and illicitly eating them was probably a corresponding pleasure.[26]

It is difficult to estimate the amount of food obtained by the nobility and higher gentry by hunting. Peasants were, by law, forbidden to hunt larger animals. No layman with an income of less than 40s. (£2) per year, or priest receiving less than 10s. per year, was allowed to keep hunting dogs, nor were they entitled to use 'fyrets, heys, nets, harepipes nor cords nor other engines for to take or destroy deer, hares nor conies nor other gentlemens game'. If they had and been caught, the penalty was a year's imprisonment.[27] That the 'gentlemen' did a considerable amount of hunting is known, but the results are not always clear. Some estimate can be obtained from the amount of game, such as venison, recorded as eaten in various rolls of household expenses. For example, Bishop Richard de Swinfield frequently dined on it, and not only at great feasts, although it was particularly prominent then. At Christmas 1289 he and his household fed on, *inter alia*, four does, and on Ascension Day 1290 they had two sides and one haunch of hart, one side of doe, one fresh deer and two roe deer, one of which was a present. Venison represented about half of the meat (including poultry) eaten at Ascension and about a quarter of that consumed at Christmas. For Easter 1290 they ate three deer from store (that is salted, as was some of the Ascension venison), which represented about one-fifth of the meat. Some of the venison was probably taken from animals in the various deer parks owned by Swinfield, rather than hunted in the strict sense. Some deer parks could contain a considerable number of deer. In the early thirteenth century the royal deer park at Havering was able to maintain more than 500 deer, and in the same period, over twenty-nine years, about 1600 deer were killed or taken alive from this park. These were not hunted but taken from a maintained stock. The bishop's deer were certainly hunted, and he and his household ate the resulting fresh venison. The household accounts, in the winter months particularly, frequently mention this venison. Boar were also hunted well into the seventeenth century. Boar's head and braun (made from the meat) were very popular at Christmas, although by the sixteenth century domesticated boar had to be used to keep up with the demand. Falconry was also very popular, although there is some evidence that the numbers of birds caught were not commensurate with the effort involved. In the Swinfield household, for example, although a good number of partridge were eaten, there is no reference to other wildfowl (such as heron, snipe and plover) which played a prominent part in large banquets of other nobility throughout this period (see Chapter 4). [28]

Fish were a very important part of the diet of all classes in the Middle Ages, and the catching and breeding of fish was a correspondingly significant factor in the economy. Demand was always high throughout the year since, before the

Reformation, everyone was expected to fast, that is eat only fish in Lent and all Wednesdays (until the fifteenth century), Fridays and Saturdays, as well as on the eve of important feasts such as Christmas. For understandable reasons no fish was eaten on the other days (except on feast days), only meat, and there were few days when both meat and fish were eaten. This was reinforced by the physicians who ordained that it was bad to eat both in the same meal. Fridays (and the vigils of some religious feasts) were supposed to be fast days, and only lunch was eaten, however most laymen did not observe this restriction. Fish formed an important part of the total food intake. Both fresh-water and sea fish were eaten and there seems to have been no difficulty in organizing the transport of fresh sea fish over the whole country, since it was available virtually anywhere. For example, the market regulations for the city of Coventry show that fresh sea fish were an important commodity there in the fifteenth and sixteenth centuries. Pershore Abbey, Worcestershire, bought some fresh sea fish from Coventry in 1381–2, and Bicester Priory, Oxfordshire, was buying a wide variety of fresh fish in Bicester, Oxford and Wantage markets in the thirteenth century: herrings, mullet, plaice, whiting, haddock, mackerel, milwell, ling and oysters. Nowhere in England is too far from the sea, and live fish could be transported for quite long distances packed in wet grass or rushes, particularly in cold weather.[29]

Most of the fish eaten were salt-water varieties. The larger part of these came from the east coast ports, such as Great Yarmouth which was one of the most important, at least up to the mid- fourteenth century. Most of the fish were herring, of which very large amounts were eaten. Every existing source that gives details of diet mentions herring very frequently, salted and smoked as well as fresh. These were bought in barrels of up to about seven hundred packed in salt. Before being put in the barrels the fish were gutted and soaked in brine for 14 to 15 hours. Because herring is a fatty fish it could not be dried, like cod, owing to the fat becoming rancid. 'Red' herrings were also bought. These were soaked in brine as for 'white' herring and then hung up to smoke for many hours. They did not keep as well as the white and were usually sold in smaller quantities. As examples of the amounts bought, Durham Priory purchased 242,000 in 1307–8 and 60,000 in 1333–4 (in the fifteenth century Durham Priory was feeding about three hundred people, including about seventy monks). These herrings were presumably salted. In Bromhead Priory, Norfolk, in 1415/16, 17 per cent of the total food expenditure was on herring.[30] Religious houses sometimes went considerable distances to purchase their fish. Up to the fourteenth century Beaulieu Abbey had its own fish-drying and kippering depot at Great Yarmouth, and regularly sent its own ship there to collect consignments of herring. Boxley Abbey, Kent, was buying herring from Berwick-on-Tweed in 1225. In 1265 a lay household, that of the Countess of Leicester, ate from 400 to 1,000 herrings a day during Lent.

South coast ports were equally important for the purchase of fish. Canterbury Cathedral Priory, in 1451, bought herring from Folkestone (10,000 fresh for the monks, 5,600 salted for the servants), as well as 400 greenfish (probably in this instance fresh fish, perhaps cod, although green fish could mean cod stored in salt), and casks of salmon and sturgeon. Much fish was also imported through Southampton. Conger eel, too, was recorded.[31] Places farther round the coast also had their fisheries. Beaulieu Abbey had a fish-drying station at St Keverne, Cornwall, in 1240, and the Canons of Torre Abbey had fishing rights in Tor Bay from their foundation in 1196. By the fifteenth century a group of new settlements was developed in the south west: Mevagissey, Newquay, Bude and Gorran Haven are all mentioned in this context. Not all sea fish were caught by deep-sea fishermen; some were trapped in sea ponds built in estuaries as fresh-water fish were caught in weirs in the rivers.[32]

Another port through which large amounts of fish (and much else) was imported was Bristol. Much of their fish came from Ireland and Iceland with whom Bristol did much trade. From Ireland came herring, mostly salted, and considerable quantities of 'salt fish', probably cod. Much of the fish from Iceland was stockfish (dried cod). Records of some of the cargoes from Iceland indicate the vast amounts of fish that were needed to keep the population supplied. In one day in August 1461, three ships docked from which were landed not less than 1 million stockfish.[33] To the even greater port of London came stockfish from the Baltic, and herrings and other fish from Flanders. In one case in 1480 three ships were loaded completely with eels. Herring and other fish were also sent to London from the east coast ports such as Newcastle, Great Yarmouth, York and Grimsby, who did their own trade in fish and much else with the Baltic ports, which included Norway and Denmark. Whales, porpoises, sturgeon and seals were also caught and eaten. The first three of these were royal fish wherever taken, but this right was not always enforced and the tenant of the land on which a whale came ashore was often granted the carcass, apart from the tongue which was a delicacy. The tenant could then salt down the meat and sell it. Whale and porpoise had to be very well cooked when roasted to make them edible.[34]

Shellfish, too, were popular. There is evidence that the collection of oysters, mussels, cockles and winkles was organized on a commercial scale, at least by the end of the tenth century. Oysters were eaten fairly frequently, mussels less so, and cockles and winkles probably fairly rarely. The shells of oysters appear frequently in archaeological records, but the shells of other fish much less so.[35] Shellfish probably formed a significant part of the diet of peasants living on the coast, for they were easily collected and the keeping of them was not controlled as with other foodstuffs.

Fresh-water fish were another important part of the fish diet. Many of these were caught in fish weirs (that is fish traps of some form in rivers). They were so common that in some instances they obstructed navigation. By law a licence was needed before a weir could be constructed. They were so efficient that too many depleted the fish stocks, but this did not stop many landowners, both religious and lay, from constructing illegal weirs. Laws were passed at regular intervals, starting in 1224–5 and continuing into the sixteenth century, but they had little effect or the repetition would not have been needed. As late as 1532 the York City Corporation was fulminating against the many fish garths (large fish traps) in the River Ouse.[36] The amount of fish obtained from these sources was often considerable – enough for such operations to be considered fishing industries. Sometimes fish-curing facilities were set up on the spot in order to deal with the fish caught. Such operations were a valuable source of income, either through the sale of fish or by the owner renting out fishing rights, or both. It is difficult to estimate the quantities of fish obtained, but it appears that the number of eels at least could, on occasion, be very large. The Domesday Book records that Evesham Abbey had one-and-a-half fisheries on the Severn which yielded 2,000 eels, and that another 2,000 eels were received from two mills on the River Avon. Eel traps were frequently set in mill streams. Eels were also often eaten salted. Other 'natural' sources of fresh fish for those lucky enough to possess them were natural ponds and marshes. Many monasteries were well placed in this way, for example those in the fenland and the Somerset levels, of which Thorney and Glastonbury Abbeys, respectively, are well known. The fisheries on these sites were sometimes very productive and valuable.[37]

The best-known source of fish in the Middle Ages is the monastic fish pond. These were certainly not restricted to religious owners, since most sizeable manors had one. Originally they were just simple stews (holding ponds) to keep live fish before they were eaten. Later much more elaborate systems were developed, linked by sluices, leats and spillways, and usually connected to a stream or river. They were well constructed, clay- or timber-lined and frequently with the water channels made of stone. They needed to be sturdy, since sometimes a considerable volume of water was penned up behind a dam or sluice. In one recorded instance, at Hailes Abbey, Gloucestershire, a sluice burst sending a flood through the abbey buildings. These complex systems were probably rarely (if ever) used to breed fish, but were generally used as rearing ponds for young fish. This provided a far larger yield than if the fish had been allowed to grow in natural conditions in rivers. The ponds were also used to store the fish before they were eaten.[38]

Many types of fish were kept in these fish ponds. Bream and pike were common, and were sometimes deliberately housed together to keep down the number of bream which tend to breed freely. Roach, perch, trout and occasionally tench were reared also. The popular belief that the monastic fish pond was stocked exclusively with carp throughout the Middle Ages is not borne out, since carp were not introduced into England until about the last quarter of the fifteenth century. Once introduced, however, they were used extensively, since they are ideal fish for this purpose. They are easy to feed and grow well on the natural pond organisms they pick up. The ponds of the London Charterhouse were reputed to have yielded no less than three hundred carp per year. These fish could be obtained from what must, in effect, have been fish nurseries. These seem to have been places where quite large numbers of fish could be bought. For example, in 1250 the sheriff of Cambridgeshire was authorized to buy 3,000 pike to stock the king's stews at Havering, and in 1265 the Constable of Windsor was ordered to provide 300 pike, together with 300 dace and roach for the stew in the park at Windsor. Live fish, as many as thirty, particularly pike and bream, were given regularly by the king to favourites. These fish were transported safely and in good condition, perhaps by some such method as described above. [39]

TWO

FOOD OF THE COUNTRYMAN

The producers of much of the food (described in Chapter 1) were the peasants who lived in the countryside. What kind of meals did they eat themselves? Even the moderately poor seem to have had about enough to eat, except in times of famine which naturally affected their class the most. Their economy was always finely balanced and very susceptible to fluctuations due to such events as bad harvests or accidents. The state of the harvest – large or small, early or late – would always have been important. Most peasants would have had little surplus above their immediate needs and a succession of bad harvests, such as occurred in 1315/1325, could and did cause disaster. Many of them would probably have been on the edge of undernourishment for most of their lives. The basic diet of the peasant consisted of carbohydrates in the form of grain, mostly barley and oats, which were baked or brewed into bread and ale. Protein, in the form of meat and eggs, was in shorter supply, particularly in the earlier part of this period, the thirteenth century.[1] Some fruit and vegetables (such as beans and onions) would have been included in the diet. Not all of the food of the country dweller was grown;

some was bought, in most cases in the ubiquitous fairs and markets which were frequently held in towns.

In the thirteenth and fourteenth centuries most peasants were subsistence farmers, growing crops such as grain, peas and beans to feed themselves and their stock. Later, many of them were waged workers on a larger farm owned by someone else. How far the majority were above mere subsistence level is unknown, but a holding of about 20 acres (which many had) is generally accepted as being enough to raise the holder above that level. Bennett calculated that this would have been sufficient to give about 153 bushels of a crop of oats, barley and wheat. He further calculated that, if the wheat was sold (as it usually would have been, if only to raise money to pay rent), this would have raised a sum of about 35s. 4d. (£1.77), taking the average price of wheat between 1260 and 1400. This sum would be correct for most of the fifteenth century, too, since prices did not rise significantly until the sixteenth century. The money obtained by selling produce would have been used for purchasing necessities. The barley and oats would have been consumed as bread or ale. The latter was usually made from barley, although it could be made from other grains (see Chapter 1). In Bolton Priory, for example, so little barley was grown that most of the canons' ale was made from oats. Even the poorer peasants would have had a garden or croft in which to grow some corn or vegetables, including those who lived mainly on wages as a shepherd or ploughman for the lord of the manor. A garden and one or two acres of land were usually thought to be just enough for one person to live on. This was certainly the view after the enclosures of the common lands, although it has been said that at least five acres (and up to ten) were necessary to grow the thirty-six bushels of corn (or its equivalent) needed to feed a family for one year. Most of this grain would have been used to make bread, the staple item of food. It seems very likely that much of that eaten by the poorer peasant would have been rye bread. It seems unlikely that every household baked bread. Possession of an oven was rare (judging by archaeological evidence), and those without ovens probably asked neighbours or used the communal oven. It has been suggested, in fact, that, except in the south of England, the consumption of bread was rare and that cereals were eaten as the staple diet chiefly in the form of porridge and broths. Children were certainly given porridge made from grain and milk.[2]

There are several descriptions in contemporary poems of food eaten by peasants. There is a list of the food eaten by the shepherds in the Shepherds play in the Chester Mystery Cycle. This consisted of bread, bacon, onions, garlic, leeks, butter and green (fresh) cheese. To this was added ale, hot meat (apparently supplied as part of their wages), a pudding (type unspecified), a 'jannock' (an oat cake), a sheep's head soused in ale and sour milk (that is curds). Another of the shepherds added to this fairly large amount of food a pig's foot (apparently originally part of a sausage mixture) and a third added smoked ham, other meat and another pudding.[3] This list probably dates back to the origin of the play cycle, early in the fourteenth century, and may have been intended to describe the usual food of shepherds at that time.

Another list occurs in Langland's *Piers the Plowman* as a description of food given to the character 'Hunger' by the poor man Piers and his neighbours. Piers first of all described the food that he had in his cottage: two green cheeses, some curds and cream, an oat cake, and two loaves of bran and beans. He also has parsley, leeks and much cabbage, but no money with which to buy pullets, no eggs and no salt meat. His neighbours, however, manage to supply much more:

Alle the poure peple then peescoddes brought
Benes and baken apples thei brouhte in here lappes
Onions and pot herbs and ripe chiries many
And profred Peers this present to plese therwith Hunger
Al Hunger eet in hast and axed after more
Thanne poure folke for fere fedde Hunger quickly
With grene leeks and peas to poysoun Hunger thei thought
. . . and fedde hunger with the best
With good ale . . .

Other poor people, described by William Langland, found that even bread and 'penny ale' were a luxury in winter, and cold meat and fish so rare as to be quite unknown. Very poor peasants ate 'wortes flechles wroughte' (that is vegetables cooked without meat) and drank water, or perhaps, if better off, bacon rind and beans.[4] The bread mentioned by the first shepherd (see above) was probably made from the grain mixture known as 'maslin' (see Chapter 1): a mixture of wheat and rye, but it could have been barley bread or one of the coarser brown breads eaten by the poor. After bad harvests, and perhaps regularly in the case of the very poor, bread made from bean flour and wheat sievings was eaten. The large quantities of bacon eaten would have come from the pig that most country people (and many town people) would have kept. The animal fed on what scraps they could spare and what it could find for itself. When it was fully grown it would have been slaughtered to feed its owners. Apparently even the very poor ate bacon, at least occasionally, as described in Chaucer's *Nun's Priest's Tale*. Here the diet of the poor widow and her two daughters was said to include milk, brown bread, bacon and an occasional egg. The widow seems to have been only relatively poor, however, since she owned three pigs, three cows and a sheep, as well as, presumably, hens.[5] It seems likely that many of the real poor usually ate little more than bread and onions, and perhaps a green vegetable such as cabbage, washed down with water. Richer villagers, probably over half of the total, kept a cow to provide them with dairy produce. It is not clear how much milk was drunk by those not keeping a cow, nor how much meat was eaten by those that did. A few sheep for milk and cheese were also sometimes kept.

One way in which the villagers made sure of a regular source of food as they grew older and less able to look after themselves was to pass the holding over to the heir while they were still alive, on condition that they were kept in food and clothing and given somewhere to live for the rest of their lives. In this way they were able to arrange for their 'retirement'. Such agreements sometimes specified in some detail the amount or varieties of food that was to be supplied. In a similar way monasteries sold (or gave) corrodies which were based on ration scales similar to those of the monastery servants. These agreements thus give an idea of the diet expected for reasonably well-to-do peasants, as do the more lavish private agreements. Often the amount of grain to be given once a year, or even once a quarter, was specified. For example, in 1294 one couple was to be given seven quarters of grain for the year, made up of three quarters of wheat, a quarter and a half of barley, a quarter and a half of beans and peas and a quarter of oats. Many other similar agreements are known, which give the recipients enough grain to eat, perhaps as bread or soups, and to make ale from to give them a reasonable diet. The quantities involved were sometimes large enough to represent a large part of the produce of the land handed over. In 1281 one widow was also to be given 5s. in cash at Pentecost and a house was to be built for her. Other agreements specified that the income from a number of animals, for example a cow, four sheep and a pig, was to be devoted to the clothing and footware of the 'pensioner'. Many of these people were thus apparently well catered for. Some of the agreements would have given a much less adequate supply of food (for example, supplying less than eight bushels of grain per year), thus forcing the old people to glean or beg in order to supplement their diet. These peasants would have drunk water more often than ale. It is not known whether such arrangements were always adhered to. Thus for some it may have been a very precarious 'retirement'.[6]

The reference to pot herbs in the extract from *Piers the Plowman* (see above) serves to illustrate that soup was a popular item of food. Soup seems to have been made from most things, particularly beans, peas and oats, flavoured with herbs: 'potage is made of the lyquor in the whiche flesshe is soden in, with puttyng to chopped herbes, and otemel and salt'. Broths were apparently sometimes also made with 'honny soppes' ('soppes' were pieces of toasted bread), and 'pease potage' was thought in the sixteenth century to be better for the health. 'Porreys' (stewed vegetables such as peas, onions or leeks and seasonings), were also popular. In the fifteenth century, a housekeeper in an almshouse in Higham Ferrers, Northamptonshire, was directed to make a mess of pottage for each inmate, using the meat that each one had brought.[7] Manorial servants were often fed very well. On at least one manor, in 1272, they fed on beef and ale, both largely provided from home-killed or home-brewed stock, fish in the form of herrings and cod, cheeses, and pottage made from peas and beans. Their bread was made from both rye and wheat. Other records show such food was distributed during the day. In 1289 carters on Ferring Manor, Sussex, had a morning meal of rye bread with ale and cheese; at noon they received bread, ale and a dish of fish or meat; and in the evening they were given a drink only. The main meal was, however, more usually given in the evening. Later servants, in this case clerks and the yeomen of the household in the Northumberland Household in 1512, received for breakfast on meat days a loaf of household bread, a bottle of beer and a piece of boiled beef. The porters and stable staff in the same household received a loaf of the same bread and a quart of beer. On fish days the clerks and yeomen received a piece of salt fish instead of the beef. It appears that at other meals they probably had much the same food as their fellows of 230 years before, except that on 'flesh days' the meat given was beef not bacon. Even so they were probably not as well fed as the fourteenth-century yeoman described in *How the Plowman learnt his Paternoster*. This man had in his hall bacon flitches, eggs, cheese, butter, milk, cream, onions, garlic, and malt to make ale.[8]

Beans and peas were a common item in the diet. These were usually eaten dried, or fresh when young. The dried crops were eaten sometimes as bread, soup or as as a kind of porridge. They were an important part of the diet of most peasants, perhaps particularly of the poorest who were allowed to pick from their neighbour's crops for a short time in the season. This privilege could mean that they gained a full week's suppers at this time. Another important right that was sometimes granted to the very poor, and routinely to the young, the old and the sick, was to glean the wheat and other grain fields after harvest. No able-bodied man who was fit to earn wages by farmwork was allowed to glean. A considerable amount could sometimes be gained by gleaning, and on occasion the women of the richer families would glean illegally. In a good field it could pay more than actually helping with the harvest, for which a woman could receive 1*d*. a day.[9]

Some of the shepherds' food (see above) was provided by their employer as part of their wages. Such a procedure was common in all walks of life. The rest of the wages would be in cash, perhaps 3*s*. (15p) per year for such employees as shepherds, ploughmen and carters. These men sometimes had the privilege of eating in the hall with the lord when he was in residence on the manor. The food given to the staff of the lord (the *famuli*) was sometimes in the form of wheat or other grain. Bennett analysed many manorial accounts and showed that the usual amount given was about one quarter of grain every twelve weeks or so. This amounts to about thirty-six bushels a year of, usually, rye or barley. This allocation would have been used to feed the whole family of the recipient. If the grain was wheat, few peasants would have been so extravagant as to eat wheat bread regularly and so would probably have sold it to buy cheaper grain. Staff at Bolton Priory received ninety-two bushels of oats, a very cheap grain, because this was the one of which they produced by far the most. It has been calculated that, on some monastic estates, staff received about 30 per cent of their wages as corn livery. This was sometimes commuted to a monetary payment when the price of corn was high, or cheaper grain was substituted.[10] Sometimes a Christmas meal was provided for a villein, for example to one of the lord's shepherds. In one case it was recorded that a man also received a loaf for his dog on Christmas Day. At Christmas in 1314 in North Curry, Somerset, three privileged tenants of the manor received two white loaves, a mess of beef and bacon with mustard, thick chicken soup, a cheese and as much ale as they could drink in the day. This last was doubtless taken as a challenge. Sometimes a piece of land was allocated to the *famulus* (employee) on which he could grow food.[11]

Another way in which country dwellers obtained food was in 'boon work'. This was work required by the lord of the manor from his tenants during ploughing or to help bring in the harvest, and it was at least partly paid for in food. The amount and type of food was often laid down in the rules and regulations governing life on the manor. It was often generous in quantity, particularly at harvest time when much heavy work was required. In one instance in the thirteenth century, at Bishopstone, Suffolk, the lord of the manor promised to give meat and ale on the first of the required days, presumably with bread, and fish and ale on the second, during the ploughing season. Those who had brought a team of oxen to the ploughing were allowed to eat supper at the lord's house. At harvest time on the first of the days required the dinner consisted of soup, wheat bread (as much as they wished to eat), beef and cheese, with as much ale as they pleased. It is easy to imagine that work after dinner was much more cheerful than before, certainly in those manors where minstrels were allowed to play, as at the manor of Hornchurch, in Essex, in 1403 and 1404. On the second day fish replaced the beef. Supper consisted of bread and cheese again with as much ale as desired on the first day, and just a loaf of bread on the second. At the end of the twelfth century an even more generous lord, the Abbot of Titchfield, gave a food supply of two kinds during the day: flesh or fish, together with bread, ale or cider and broth. For supper the lucky tenants were given a meal of a fish (which could be a whole mackerel) and a wheaten loaf of 40 oz (or a barley loaf on a second day). On some manors the bread was rye only. The type and size was strictly laid down in the record of manorial customs (see below). The soup was usually only a gruel without any meat in it.[12] Sometimes only water was provided as a drink in a so-called 'dry boon'. When ale (or sometimes cider) was provided the boon was known as a 'wet boon'. Occasionally villagers had the right to bring a comrade to the second and third of a series of boons. This food was a valued part of life. It had to be provided on a generous scale since the peasants had to put off their own work to carry out the lord's work, and they sometimes refused to help if food was not provided. In 1291 the villeins of the manor of Broughton went on strike because they said the loaves given to them were not as large as custom said they should be. The court investigating the case found that the loaves did not need to be bigger than those normally purchased if the lord, the Abbot of Ramsey, so wished and that two men should share a three-farthing loaf between them, that is one weighing perhaps 2 lb. Sometimes the lord provided a whole sheep for all of those who had given service. In one case in Barton in the Clay, Bedfordshire, the sheep was given to them alive and they were only to have it if they could catch it.[13]

The giving of food was not restricted to that from the lord to his tenants. At Christmas it was frequently the custom for each tenant to give to the lord a hen (partly as payment for being allowed to keep poultry), or sometimes grain which was brewed into ale. At Easter they would give eggs, and sometimes received a meal from their lord in return. At Christmas also the lord was expected to give his tenants a meal, for example bread, cheese, pottage and two dishes of meat. The tenant might be directed to bring his own plate, mug and napkin if he wished there to be a cloth on the table, and a faggot of brushwood to cook his food, unless he wished to have it raw.[14] Sometimes the custom said explicitly that the lord had to give a Christmas meal because the tenant had given him the food. In at least one instance the value of the food to be provided by the lord was to be to the same value as that given by the tenant. The role of the lord in this case appears to have been merely to organize the village Christmas dinner. The value of the dinner was not always so finely balanced as this however: sometimes the lord gained, sometimes the tenant. These customs were maintained for several centuries, lasting in some cases after the end of the manorial system when compulsory work had been commuted into the paying of rent. Workers employed on a more casual basis would not necessarily have been so well placed. Thus a labourer employed on the building of Vale Royal Abbey, Cheshire, in 1278–79 could only have earned enough in a year (assuming that he worked every day, except holidays, and that the price of grain did not rise too high) to buy enough to provide a minimally nutritious diet of barley for a family of four. Extra money from other sources, or food from a land holding, would have been essential to provide additions to a very monotonous diet. Skilled workers would have been considerably better off.[15]

The food of the villager was supplemented by fruit grown in the garden. Cherries, apples (both mentioned by Piers the Plowman above) and pears were commonly eaten, plums perhaps slightly less so. Nuts also were grown, including filberts, walnuts and sweet chestnut. The diet also included vegetables (mentioned above) and pot herbs, such as parsley, and others used to add flavour to sauces and stews. This food was accompanied by what could be gathered in the woods and hedges or caught, such as small birds and rabbits. Fishing, for fresh-water or salt fish, also helped provide extra food. On some manors men paid a small sum for the right to fish in some of the manorial waters, while others provided a 'common water' for fishing. Sometimes men poached fish. It must have been very tempting and not too difficult to take fish illegally. A large fish, for example a salmon or large tench, would have made a considerable addition to the diet of a villager. Poaching was sometimes on a very large scale, as in 1376 when sixty people were accused of taking thirty deer and a fish worth 100s. (£5.00) from the park of Evesham Abbey. Poaching of larger animals, such as deer, is also revealed by bones found in excavations in one forest village in Northamptonshire.[16]

Shellfish too were sought by those who lived on the coast. Children were frequently sent on gathering errands, and sometimes died while doing so: in 1357 a twelve-year-old was washed out to sea off the Lincolnshire coast and drowned while collecting cockles. The food of the peasant family was also supplemented by hens' eggs, and in some cases the butter and cheese made by the women, who were also among the chief gatherers of wild produce. Honey, the chief source of sweetness, came from beehives, probably also looked after by the women. The diet described here changed little throughout the Middle Ages, up to the sixteenth century. There was, however, a general increase in prosperity after the Black Death (which caused many changes in the countryside), reflected in a generally more plentiful diet. This is evident from the more generous liveries given to some *famuli* and meals provided for harvest workers. In 1397 some of these received herrings, cheese and eggs, as well as beef and ale.[17]

Life for the villager was not entirely a round of work with no time to spare for celebration. A man who married was usually expected to give a feast to his fellow workers in which the bride ale played a large part. This bride ale was brewed for the occasion and the profits of the occasion given to the bride. Friends attending usually paid far more for the ale than was allowed commercially. 'Help ales' were held sometimes, too. These were charitable occasions on which the profits went to someone who had fallen on hard times. Funerals were also occasions for feasting and drinking. The wake was often very elaborate when someone important had died, and a number of 'poor men' would usually have been fed at such a time. On the death of the fourth Lord Berkeley in 1368, at least a hundred geese were fattened for the funeral. There were many other 'ales' held throughout the year, sometimes by, or on behalf of, the lord. Tenants were required to come to these 'scot ales' (they had various other names) and pay up to 3*d*. (1p) for the privilege of drinking there. On occasion there were such pleasant customs as allowing the village bachelors to drink without payment on the last day of a 'scot ale' as long as they could stand. If they sat down they had to pay. The Church generally frowned on these occasions and on visits to the village alehouse, since drunkeness was the usual result. Other feasts were organized at the end of ploughing (at least in the sixteenth century) when seed cake, pasties and 'furmentie' (unground, hulled wheat boiled in almond milk) were enjoyed. Parish guilds, too, usually held a banquet on the feast day of their patron saint.[18]

THREE

FOOD OF THE TOWN DWELLER

The inhabitants of towns had a far wider choice of food, although, as always, the resources of the buyer limited what could actually be provided. Considerable amounts of food were needed to supply large towns. It has been calculated, for example, that if the population of London in 1300 was between eighty and one hundred thousand, as is now believed to have been the case, more than 1 million bushels of grain of various kinds (that is well over 20,000 tons) were probably consumed by the people each year. As well as this they probably used up to 100,000 tons of wood to cook this food.[1] Most of the grain came from the London hinterland (the counties around the City), and it seems probable that, by 1300 there were many manors that were at least partly devoted to supplying London with its needs. The grain (wheat, barley – sometimes in the form of malt – and oats) seem to have come from what could be called an 'outer ring', Oxfordshire and Kent for example, much of this bulky material being transported by water where possible.

Live cattle and fresh meat were also brought to London from surrounding counties, such as Essex, to supply the City with meat. Live poultry, too, were probably driven in, as they were later, in the nineteenth century. The demand for beef in London was greater than could be met from the arable land of the south of England, and the same applied to the meat supply of other large towns. Some cattle were therefore driven long distances to market. For example, in the thirteenth century they came to Gloucester from South Wales. Sheep were later also driven to towns in the same way. The number of animals needed in a large town was enormous. In fourteenth-century Florence the annual consumption of the population of 90,000 was 4,000 oxen and calves, 60,000 sheep, 20,000 goats and 30,000 pigs. The smaller animals, such as pigs, were often raised in the city, and seem commonly to have roamed the streets to the great annoyance of all. Presumably these animals were single beasts being raised by householders for slaughter when they were old enough. There was a piggery at Westminster Abbey which occasionally sold surplus beasts on the open market. Items such as rabbits, swans, venison and pike were also imported for the much smaller luxury market.[2]

There was also a demand for dairy products, such as butter and cheese, and these too were brought into London from the surrounding counties. Much came from Essex and Suffolk. Essex cheeses were famous, being produced in enormous round 'weys' of several hundred pounds in weight. Probably less milk would have been imported since it would not have travelled as well as butter (which could be salted for this purpose) and cheese. It is noticeable that milk was not mentioned in the City records as are most other foods. Cheese was available in four main varieties: hard (probably of a cheddar type), soft (or cream cheese), green cheese (a very new soft cheese) and 'spermyse' (cream cheese flavoured with herbs). The quality of dairy products in general was probably very variable. It is possible that well-off households kept their own cows, and were thus able to supply their own needs and perhaps those of their neighbours. Certainly cows and ewes were frequently leased for an annual sum to individuals who consumed their produce. Others were able to buy dairy products from a local farm, as did John Stow in the mid-sixteenth century. As a youth, Stow bought his milk from a farm belonging to the nuns of the Minories at a rate of 3 pints for ½d. in the summer and 2 pints for ½d. in the winter.[3]

Counties near London supplied market garden produce, although much fruit- and vegetable-growing also took place in the suburbs of the city. There were many gardens in the City belonging to large houses, and, after these had supplied their household, the surplus fruit and vegetables were sold. Some seem to have sold most of their produce to the markets. There was quite a large trade in the selling of garden produce. Until 1345 the gardeners had apparently stood in front of the Church of St Austin, by the side of the gate of St Paul's churchyard, selling 'pulse, cherries, vegetables and other wares to their trade pertaining', but such had been the clamour this large number of traders had caused that the priests in St Austin's Church could not hear themselves singing mass. Also the gardeners prevented people from getting into and out of the church. They were therefore moved to a space on the south side of St Paul's churchyard. The variety of goods available was large and included all garden fruit, such as apples, pears, cherries and nuts, as well as vegetables, including onions, leeks (very large quantities of these, because they were popular both as vegetables and for flavouring), beans, cabbages, turnips, parsnips, beet (probably grown for its leaves rather than for the root), radishes and carrots. The carrots were not all orange in colour; they also came as purple, yellow and white. Vine fruits, too, were grown, from which large amounts of verjuice (for pickling and cooking) were made. Quinces, peaches, mulberries and medlars (like apples) were also grown and sold to the rich.[4]

Growing food in town gardens appears to have been much the same, and as prone to misfortune, as it is today. For example, caterpillars ate the cabbages, and lettuces came up thickly and had to be thinned out as they grew. Different varieties of cabbage and greens, including spinach, were grown and were planted to crop at different times of the year. Many herbs of different kinds were grown to add to the pottage, such as sage, mint, fennel, parsley, marjoram, orach, borage, sorrel and basil, and many others including some now not regarded as herbs. Some (such as lettuce) are now regarded as salad vegetables, to be eaten raw, rather than pot herbs, or they are used in either role (such as parsley). Others (such as pimpernel, primrose and groundsel) would now not be regarded as edible at all. Sophisticated grafting, of cherries or plums on a vine stock, or a vine stock on a cherry, for example, was carried out regularly. Commercial orchards played some part in the provision of fruit to the town markets. Orchards existed in the Romford area, Essex, from the early sixteenth century, although commercial vegetable growing came later in the 1560s. A garden in Cuxham, Oxfordshire, was planted with 169 fruit trees, probably all apples, in 1303. Apples, pears, cherries and vines were grown there at other times, and apples and cider at least from its fairly large fruit production were sold.[5]

Once in the town, fruit and vegetables were sold through a large number of retail outlets: markets, fairs, shops and wandering salesmen (frequently women). The whole scene must have been noisy and chaotic. The gardeners in St Paul's churchyard, London, have already been mentioned (see above). Town and city authorities made considerable efforts to control the sale of food, wherever it was sold. Attempts were made to set a 'reasonable' price for many commodities, particularly bread and ale, the main staples of the diet. These were fixed annually by the assize of bread and ale (see below). Similar attempts were made to regulate the conditions under which food was sold. The control started before the food reached the city, with much fulmination (and regulations) against the activities of 'forestallers' – those who bought up produce before it reached the city market and then sold it to private customers.[6] The markets in a medieval town occupied an important part in the economy and were elaborately regulated. Much of the food, at least of the middle and lower classes, was purchased in markets, and in London the City authorities spent a lot of time and energy trying to make sure that goods were in general sold there and not elsewhere in the city.

The markets in London during the Middle Ages were situated on sites established mostly by the fourteenth century, with some exceptions. This was also the case with most other towns. Usually the market was an open space, or sometimes a street, devoted to selling goods, usually from temporary stalls set up and taken down each day. In larger towns there were markets for the sale of particular goods, such as grain, meat and fish. In a large town like London, some commodities had several markets devoted to their sale. Thus, among other things, meat was chiefly sold in the the 'Stokkes' (roughly on the site of the present Mansion House), and fish in Eastcheap and Old Fish Street. General goods (poultry, eggs, butter, cheese, herbs and fruit, for example) were sold in Gracechurch Street and on Cornhill. Grain was sold in the Leadenhall Market. In some cases, such as the 'Stokkes' in London, the market was (by the fifteenth century) a substantial stone building, with stalls on the ground floor and rooms to let to merchants above them. The Leadenhall market was a large, open courtyard surrounded by a building several stories high. In these places the stalls were permanent but most markets (such as Eastcheap) were street markets.[7]

Town authorities (aided, and sometimes impeded, by the merchant companies) made a great effort to control the markets, their hours, prices, quality of the food, the conditions and who sold what and where. By means of official sealed weights and measures they kept an eye on the accuracy of the quantity of goods bought. They also tried to prevent engrossing (that is cornering the market in goods to sell later at a high price) by making regulations, such as those at York which insisted that all food brought to York from the surrounding countryside was sold in the Thursday market. This also aided the checking of standards. Another practice that town authorities frowned on was the uncontrolled selling of goods in the street by wandering salesmen. In 1345 in London, for example, a proclamation was made on behalf of the men of the poultry trade. This concerned the many traders who were bringing their poultry to London to sell, and doing so in the lanes and houses of their hosts and elsewhere. The proclamation forbade the practice and ordered that the poultry was brought to Leadenhall Market to sell. Once in the market these traders (and others) were forbidden to sell to cooks and 'regrators' (resellers) before the 'hour of prime' (6.00 a.m.). They could sell to anyone for private consumption before this. Freemen of London sold their poultry in the Poultry Market. Regulations generally differed for non-citizens, or 'foreigners', and efforts were made to see that those claiming the privileges of citizens, with all that this meant in terms of greater freedom for selling goods, actually did reside in the city and not at 'country houses' outside. Such was the case with certain butchers who rented houses in Stratford, well outside the city of London boundaries.[8]

Town and city authorities also made efforts to control the environmental problems that arose. These were posed by the large numbers of traders selling such perishable goods as meat and fish, which produced large amounts of by-products in the form of entrails. For example, the butchers in the London Shambles, near Newgate, made a great nuisance of themselves in the fourteenth century by using a quay on the

River Fleet to clean the entrails of the beasts they had slaughtered. They were in the practice of throwing these entrails onto the pavement outside the house of the Grey Friars. Attempts were made to force them to clean the entrails elsewhere, but without success. The butchers, with the exception of those in Eastcheap and the Stocks, were eventually forbidden to slaughter beasts in the City. Butchers seem to have frequently caused this kind of problem. In Winchester in the fourteenth century they treated their offal in much the same way. One of them was actually accused of slaughtering a cow outside his shop in the high street. Similarly, cooks were found guilty of throwing the entrails of poultry into the street in Coventry in the fifteenth century.[9]

The fishmongers seem in general to have caused less of this kind of nuisance, apart from washing their fish in the common conduit (see below). They sold a very large variety of sea fish including cod, conger, dory, turbot, bass, mullet and lamprey. Roach, barbel and dace were included among the fresh-water kinds. This range was perhaps rather larger than in many other places. Obviously London was exceptional in that a greater effort was made to supply such a large market, but most sea ports (such as Great Yarmouth, a centre of the herring fishing industry) would have had a reasonable variety available. Inland towns, too, had fresh salt and fresh-water fish for sale (see above p.20). Dried or salted fish were similarly easily available. Large amounts of 'stockfish' (dried cod) and salted and pickled herrings were imported. Most towns would have had fresh-water fish caught in the neighbourhood. They were caught in the London City ditch in the sixteenth century as well as from the River Thames. Shellfish, such as native oysters and mussels, were also sold in surprisingly large quantities. Both shellfish and salt fish could be sold by 'birlesters' (itinerant salesmen or women) in London in the fifteenth century. The prices of fish were very variable and sometimes surprisingly cheap. For example, in 1382 herrings from Scotland and Great Yarmouth were ordered to be sold at six for 1*d*. (that is nearly twelve for 1p), and later in the same year at nine for 1*d*. Oysters were also very cheap at 4*d*. (1½p) per bushel.[10]

Bread, as an important part of the diet, was sold widely. Perhaps oddly in London, by an ordinance of 1377, bakers were forbidden to sell bread 'before their own ovens', that is from their own shops, and were supposed to sell only in the markets. This seems not to have applied in other towns. In all towns 'hucksters' (streetsellers), usually female, were allowed to sell bread from house to house. They seem to have made their profit as a result of being allowed, by law, to receive thirteen batches for every twelve bought: a 'baker's dozen'. They were supposed to sell only while passing through the streets (that is they were not supposed to stand still and sell). In Winchester and other towns, the hucksters were allowed to stand and sell their bread, but they had to pay for the privilege.[11] Bread was sold in several different varieties. The most expensive was 'paindemaigne' (bread of the Lord, that is Communion bread), known in the fifteenth century as 'manchet'. This was made from a wholemeal flour, from which much of the bran had been removed by means of sieving (or bolting) through fine cloths. It was a pale cream colour due to the wheat germ it contained, most of which is removed from today's white bread. It also contained more of the bran. Less fine flour was made by allowing more and more of the bran to pass the sieving process, and loaves were made from these flours of increasing shades of colour. They bore many names, depending on the degree of fineness, such as 'wastel', 'bis' (or 'trete'), 'cocket' and just white. This last was apparently common, white bread, not 'paindemaigne'. The brownest bread, made from unbolted flour, was known as 'tourte' (or *panis integer*). The names tourte, bis and cocket may have been applied also to the very dark rye bread. One other type of flour used was maslin, from the mixture of rye and wheat with that name.[12]

According to the Assize of Bread and Ale (for ale see below), made originally by Henry III in 1266, a loaf was supposed to sell for 1*d*., the size varying according to the price of grain. This variation in size applied to bread of all types, thus a farthing loaf of 'paindemaigne' would weigh half as much as a trete loaf, which in turn weighed half as much as a tourte loaf. Loaves of other qualities, such as cocket, sold at intermediate prices. In this way a poor customer could buy a loaf four times as large as that bought by a rich customer for the same price, but of poorer quality. A penny loaf was quite large, so most people, the poorer ones certainly, usually wanted smaller loaves, down to a farthing loaf. These loaves were not popular with the bakers. In Winchester, in 1366, the bakers were fined for refusing to sell farthing loaves. In London a few years later, in 1382, the City authorities went to the length of minting some farthings so that the bakers (and the brewers who had been refusing to sell a farthing's worth of ale) had no excuses for their action. In Winchester at the same time, butchers refused to sell even as small an amount as a penny's worth (that is less than about 2½ lb of meat). The enforcement of the Assise lay with the town authorities of each place, who altered the weight of the loaf as the price of grain changed. It was necessary to keep a firm control over the bakers because of their potential power: a strike by them, such as occurred in some towns, would deprive a town of its staple food.[13]

As already implied, much food was bought in shops, as well as in the markets and from hucksters. Many of these shops were grouped together, often in terraces, depending on what they sold, sometimes giving their name to a street that still exists, for example Milk Street and Bread Street in

London. Most shops were very small, some as little as 5–6 feet by 10 feet, with slightly grander ones having a frontage on the street of about 12 feet, and later sometimes even larger. In the case of the smaller shops there were generally living quarters behind, while the larger ones tended to have quarters above. The shop itself was merely a room fronted by an unglazed opening closed by a shutter. This shutter let down to form a shelf from which goods could be sold. These shops were cramped inside, and sometimes heavily stocked, so that customers must on occasion have had to stand outside on the street.[14] Some shops had a general stock, selling herrings, mustard, candles and other goods in the case of a shop on the manor in Havering in 1390–1. Other 'shops' were more like bazaars, where up to fifty traders, all selling similar goods, shared space in a large shed-like area. In the fifteenth century, outside London at least, bakers, butchers and fishmongers sold not only their own speciality, but also a wide range of other edible goods including cheese and butter. Quite a number of shops sold ready prepared food, although not ale which they and the 'piebakers' were forbidden to sell. In London there were many cookshops selling roast meat of various kinds, including roast thrush and finches, and geese, hens and capons baked in pastry. In 1378 the latter cost 8d. (3p), or 6d. without the pastry and 1½d. for 'paste, fire and trouble upon a capon', if the customer found the capon. Thrushes were three for 2d. and finches 1d. for ten. Plover, woodstock and teal were 2½d. each, but a pheasant cost 13d., heron 18d. and bittern 18d. Roast rabbit cost 4d., and 'the best lamb roasted' 7d. Sauces and puddings also were sold. These cookshops seem, originally at least, to have supplied meals in the customer's house if required. They became popular partly because many houses had no adequate kitchen or cooking facilities, and also because the best way to keep food, particularly in the summer, was to cook it. In addition they were very useful when unexpected guests had to be fed. They were mostly, at least in the twelfth and thirteenth centuries, congregated on or near the banks of the River Thames. In 1212 it was ordered that the shops should be whitewashed and plastered, and to have no internal partitions. Since this regulation was made following a disastrous fire in London, this is certainly due more to a desire to inhibit fire than to improve hygiene, which was probably, at best, very poor. There were also shops of the 'pybakers', generically known with the cooks and tavern keepers as victuallers. These were all forbidden in 1412, on the eve of various saints' days at least, to open after 10.00 p.m. (after 9.00 p.m. in 1416). In the thirteenth century and later, cooks and piebakers in London were forbidden to sell raw food (this was encroaching on the trade of the butchers, etc.) or to keep hostels for the entertainment of guests and travellers. Cookshops still remained in the fifteenth century, but there seem to have been many fewer than before judging by the poor state the 'Mistery' (Guild) of Cooks (or Pastelers) claimed to be in at the end of the century.[15] That there was considerable overlap between the various cookshops, piebakers and taverns is evident in the medieval poem 'London Lickpenny', which also gives a vivid picture of the London street scene:

> Then to Westminster gate I went
> when the sone was at highe prime
> Cokes to me they toke good intent
> called me nere for to dyne
> and proferyd me good brede ale and wyne
> a fayre clothe they began to sprede
> rybbes of befe bothe fat and fyne
> but for lacke of money I might not spede
>
> In to london I gan me hy
> of all the lond it bearethe the prise

48

hot pescods one gan cry
strabery rype and chery in the ryse
one bad me come nere and by some spice
pepar and saffron they gan me bede
clove, grayns and flowre of rise
for lacke of money I might not spede

The poor man in the poem is later also offered hot sheep's
feet, ribs of beef again, 'many a pie' and mackerel. It is not
clear whether the fish was cooked or not.[16]

The taverns undoubtedly sold food as well as drink. They
did not all lodge guests and were divided into alehouses and
those selling wines. There were probably always many
taverns in towns, although perhaps more alehouses. It seems
probable that most alehouses were traders on a very small
scale, making their own ale (or, in towns, buying it from the
brewer) and only open on an intermittent basis, particularly
in the country. In the towns there would have been larger
and more permanent establishments too. Very many of the
brewers were women (as noted above, p.6). In the fifteenth
century, for example, Fleet Street, London, was tenanted very
largely by 'alewives'. Most of the rest of the tenants were
apparently makers of felt hats. Ale was also sold by
hucksters. The small scale of the enterprises was largely due
to the fact that ale was much better consumed where it was
brewed, since it deteriorated very quickly. By the fourteenth
century at least some alehouses were quite large. One in
Paternoster Row, London, had two floors with garrets and
thirty seats on each floor. The 'Boar's Head' in King Street,
owned by Westminster Abbey, was a very splendid building at
the end of the fifteenth century. It had no less than twenty-
seven rooms by then, and outside there was a painted sign
board and a large wooden boar's head.[17] There were so many
taverns in London by the reign of Edward VI that he passed
an Act to avoid 'many inconveniences, much evil rule and

common resort of misruled persons used and frequented in many taverns of late newly set up in very great number in back lanes, corners and suspicious places within the City of London and in divers other towns and villages within this realm'. The Act went on to attempt again to regulate the prices at which various wines were sold and the amount of wine kept in private houses (see below). It apparently had no effect from the outset, probably because the Vintners had a right to open a tavern where they pleased which apparently took precedence over the Act. Certainly there are the names of more than a hundred in the City of London letter books, rather more than the number allowed by the Act, which was not repealed until the reign of James VI.

Taverns were marked with a 'bush' (a pole projecting from the building on the end of which was a bunch of leaves or sometimes a real bush). Other signs were used too. Sir John Howard ate or drank frequently at named inns when he was in London, for example the 'taverne of the Sonne' in Westminster in 1464, the 'Mermayd' in Bread Street and many others are named in his accounts. It is evident from a London ordinance of 1375 that these bushes were sometimes a great nuisance. This ordinance complained that the 'alestakes' sometimes projected so far over the highway as to impede the progress of riders. Their great weight also caused the houses to deteriorate. It was therefore ordered that no one should have an alestake projecting over the King's highway more than 7 feet 'on pain of paying 40 pence' to the Mayor and Alderman at the Guildhall. This was possibly the width of the footpath in the wider thoroughfares. The alestake also served as an announcement that a new brew had been made, and was a request for the aleconner (inspector) to come and judge the quality of the ale (see Chapter 4).[18] The measure by which ale was sold (as well as the price) was also carefully checked, probably in great part because of the important part it played as a staple beverage.

The Assise of Bread and Ale, as well as fixing the price of bread, also ruled that the price of ale should be tied to that of the grain from which it was made. Thus the volume of ale obtained for 1*d.* varied with the price of grain and so, as the Act said, if barley cost 20*d.* per quarter, then brewers in the city should be able to sell their ale at 1*d.* for 2 gallons; in the country where costs were less, at 3 or 4 gallons for 1*d.* In 1337 best ale cost 1½*d.* (1p) per gallon (in comparison sweet wine from Gascony or Spain cost 6*d.* per gallon in 1383), and the price was much the same until well into the sixteenth century. At the beginning of the fourteenth century a gallon of ale would have represented the equivalent of about two-thirds of a day's wages for a labourer. This improved later when the skilled craftsman could buy nearly three times as much as he could have a century earlier.

The chief problem with this system was that brewers and retailers did not always obey the rules. The offence was frequent and the penalty for selling ale at more than the assise price could be quite severe. In London in 1337, for example, it was ordained that the penalty for a first offence was three days in prison and a fine of 40*d.* (17p, a skilled craftsman could earn 6*d.* per day), for a second offence six days in prison and a fine of half a mark, (6*s.* 8*d.*: 33p), and for the third offence the culprit had to leave the city. Similar penalties were imposed for bakers who disobeyed the price regulations. Ale had to be sold in containers of a gallon, pottle (four pints) and quart, marked with the official seal to guarantee their accuracy. It was not to be sold in the 'hanaps' from which it was usually drunk. The same ordinance laying down the penalties for profiteering also made it clear that, as would be expected, there was more than one strength sold, at least two and possibly three. The two usual qualities were sometimes known as 'double' and 'single' (or small ale). There was no legal definition of the proper strengths of these ales (or their successor beers).

Originally the names must have arisen from the use of twice the weight of malt for one of the brews, although it could have been ale or beer made by boiling the 'wort' (extracted sugars) twice as long for one as for the other. The interpretation of strength must have varied quite considerably. In 1552 the London authorities attempted to enforce the use of twice the malt for double beer by law. The degree of success is doubtful, since by 1560 'double-double' beer was being made. This perhaps included the beers known as 'huffcap', 'mad dog', 'angel's food' and 'dragon's milk'.[19]

Water was also much used as a beverage by the poorer parts of the community, and was supplied from the conduits in various parts of towns. In London it was also supplied by water carriers who may have taken it from the relatively pure conduits or from the River Thames. These water carriers had rounds rather like a modern milkman. A continual effort had to be made by the City authorities to prevent the brewers from monopolizing the conduits as a source of good, clean water for making their ale (and the fishmongers for washing their fish; see Chapter 1). Much effort went into trying to keep public water supplies pure and usable for ordinary citizens and preventing them from being misused. The London authorities imposed a tax on carters carrying goods from ships in London docks to help pay for the removal of 'dung and other filth' in Dowgate dock. This 'filth' prevented the common water carriers from pursuing their trade.[20]

The sale of wine was as regulated, as was the sale of ale. Strictly speaking the wine sellers were supposed only to sell either white or red wine, not both. This was to inhibit the mixing of the two varieties, to which the London authorities were strongly opposed. In 1353 wine sellers were also forbidden to stock sweet wine with any other type. These prohibitions may have been partly because it was thought to be bad for the health to mix wines.[21] Probably little wine was kept in the private houses of commoners, even those who were better off. Most would buy in wine as needed for family use and that of guests, as they did food from the cookshops. Edward VI forbade any commoner to keep more than 10 gallons of wine in his house for his own private use, unless he had an income of more than 100 marks per year or property worth 1,000 marks (100 marks equalled £66 13s. 4d., the income of a fairly wealthy member of the gentry).[22]

Wine drunk in England tended to be new, and therefore strong and harsh. Less strong wines did not keep well, and no old wine was well regarded whether it was originally strong or not. Old wine must have developed a very bitter taste and considerable acidity, and it was sometimes given to the poor, who may or may not have appreciated it, or even thrown it away. There appear to have been regular sales of the King's old wines. There does seem to have been some idea that allowing air into a wine cask would cause it to go off, since the Goodman of Paris gave instructions on how to tap a cask without letting air into it (incidentally, his method would not have worked). He also gave detailed instructions on how to 'cure' bad wine (he did not say what he regarded as 'bad' wine) by letting it stand out in the frost. To prevent wine from smelling bad he suggested adding a bag of powdered elderwood and another of grain of paradise to each cask. There was thus considerable awareness of the decomposition of wine, if little idea of what to do about it.[23] Quite what was regarded as bad wine in the Middle Ages is in doubt. In the period 1289–90 in at least one noble household, that of Richard de Swinfield, wine was drunk from barrels that had been tapped up to three months beforehand. It must have been very sour, but still apparently regarded as palatable. It was not until bottled wine began to appear in the sixteenth century that this problem was overcome.[24] Wine was not usually imported in the summer months, probably due to the recognition that it would go off very quickly. The new wines from Gascony were shipped in the late autumn, arriving during the last three months of the year. Sometimes casks of unfermented grape juice were shipped with the first ships. This was apparently not very popular, although Henry III seems to have been fond of it and members of the suite of Bishop Beckington drank it in 1442, when on an embassy to negotiate a marriage between Henry VI and a daughter of the Count of Armagnac. Wine shipped in the same year in which it was made was known as the 'wine of the vintage'; wine racked off the lees in the following year and then shipped over in April, May and June was called 'wine of reck' (or variations on this). The latter was much more highly regarded since it was of higher quality.[25]

Most of the wine imported into England came from Gascony after the loss of Normandy. This Gascon wine was much cheaper than any other owing to the large amount imported, although a great deal was shipped from the other French wine-producing provinces. While the particular part of Gascony from which wine came does not in general appear to have been noted when the wine was put on sale, variations in prices do show that sometimes the better quality of wine from a particular area was taken into account. Gascon wine was generally liked because it was strong and of a good red colour. The value placed on a good colour in red wine is evident from several cases of attempts to sell dyed wine in the fifteenth and sixteenth centuries (see Chapter 4). Many instances of prosecution for mixing wines were probably due to a desire to have stronger wine, and at the same time to sell lighter and less strong wine at a better price by mixing it with Gascon wine.[26] Wine also came from Germany. This was known generically as 'Rhenish' ('Ryneys wine') and covered, up to about the end of the sixteenth century, all Alsatian, Rhenish, Moselle and other German wines. Italian wine was popular, too. Wine from Rivoglio, known as 'Riboldi' or 'Rybole', and wine from Sicily were particularly popular. Spanish wine was imported widely throughout the whole of the Middle Ages. Its strength particularly was appreciated, and in the sixteenth century it became tremendously popular. The resulting increase in imports was in the form of what was designated 'sack' (or 'seck'), a wine unknown until then. Sack seems to have been dry Spanish wine, given this name to differentiate it from the sweeter wines from elsewhere, although the name was later extended to wines from many other places – sherry sack, Madeira sack and Canary sack (this latter was sometimes known as sweet sack) – all of which were imported. Sack was frequently drunk with added sugar.[27] Sweet wines from southern Europe were popular too and were the subject of several regulations concerning how they should be sold (see Chapter 6). These wines included 'malvezyn' ('malvesie' or 'malvoisie'), a kind of malmesey from Crete, 'romeney', an inferior malmesey, and wine 'de la Rivere' from Ribera in northern Spain. There were also 'bastard' (a sweet Spanish wine), 'oseye' (sweet French, Alsatian or sometimes Spanish wine), and 'vernage' ('vernaccia'), a much esteemed sweet wine, probably from Italy.[28]

Spirits do not seem to have been sold as a drink in England, at least not in taverns. However, the distillation of wine to produce alcohol had been known in Europe since at least the twelfth century, and probably before that, since distillation as a process was known to the Greeks and Romans. Alcohol was at first used mainly as a medicine, distilled by apothecaries, but was being used in fourteenth-century England as '*Aqua vitae*' ('water of life') in recipes for spiced wine. Other recipes describe how to make a kind of liqueur by distilling 'strong wiyn' with spices. It was also used in a recipe in the cookery book ' Forme of Cury' in the same way as brandy is poured over Christmas puddings and set alight today. The manufacture of liqueur-type drinks and the mixing of herbs with wine was common, particularly in the sixteenth century, although the varieties known as 'hippocras' and 'clarre' had been used for centuries (see Chapter 6). Spirits, as such, were being drunk in Germany by the end of the fifteenth century, and probably before, to the extent that a decree of the town of Nuremberg was issued in 1496 to prevent excessive consumption. By the sixteenth century spirits were certainly being drunk in England for non-medicinal purposes and were increasing in popularity (they had been popular in Ireland much earlier). One author described spirits as 'wholsome for the stomach' and of a marvellous quality which 'chaungeth the afectione of the mind . . . taketh away sadness' and 'maketh men . . . witty'. None was apparently being imported into Scotland at the beginning of the same century.[29]

Considerable amounts of what might be called groceries, that is dried fruit and spices, were also bought and sold. Most if not all of these products would have been bought by the richer households for their elaborate banquets (see Chapter 6).[30] A picture of how a fairly wealthy townsman expected to live is given by the treatise that one of them wrote for his wife. The townsman, the Goodman of Paris or *Le Ménagier de Paris*, was a prosperous and fairly well- educated *bourgeois*, with no claim or wish to have a higher status, writing in about 1394.[31] It is obvious from what he says that he expected to be able to buy all of the wide range of foodstuffs described above, both raw and prepared in various ways. He had staff who prepared the meals, although it was up to his wife to oversee the preparation. Nothing too elaborate was expected. He admitted that some recipes from the source he used were too elaborate for the cook of a bourgeois, and he had not seen stuffed pig when he began to write. His interest in food is interestingly practical – he was someone who had knowledge of the everyday organization of meals. His practical experience is evident in the description of a feast in which he participated (see Chapter 7).[32]

From various sources it is possible to get some idea of what the average town dweller ate. The Act on the Diet and Apparel of Servants of 1363 stated the food that the servants of the nobility, artisans and tradesmen should be given daily. This consisted of meat or fish once a day, the remains of other foods, milk, cheese and 'other provisions' according to the employee's rank. 'Other provisions' must have included bread of something less than the best quality, ale, and probably also onions or leeks and cabbage, all in the form of soup. Sixteenth-century town dwellers (artificers and husbandmen, at least) ate well according to Harrison in his *Description of England* (1577). Their food consisted principally of beef, and indeed other meats, together with poultry, fruit, fruit pies, cheese, butter and eggs.[33]

The standard of living dropped during the century owing to a rise in prices. Even so, at the end of the sixteenth century charitable institutions were feeding their residents a diet much the same as the townsman above, giving them mutton, beef, whiting, herring and other fish, as well as milk and butter. In 1588 the 'House of Correction' at Bury gave 8oz of rye bread, 1 pint of porridge, ¼ lb of meat and 1 pint of beer at supper and dinner on meat days. On fish days residents received a similar meal, with the meat replaced by one good herring and ⅓ lb of cheese. Those that were willing to work received an allowance of beer and a little bread between meals. This compares well with the amount given to inmates of Sherburn Hospital (for lepers), Durham. Here each person received a loaf of bread weighing about 2½ lb and a gallon of beer each day. Meat was added to this three times a week, and cheese, herring and eggs on the other days. Butter, vegetables and salt were also provided. The statutes of the hospital stressed the need for fresh food.[34]

FOUR

FOOD OF THE GENTRY

Having seen how the great bulk of the population ate we may now turn to see how the minority, the lesser gentry, the nobility, the royal court and the Church fared. This is a considerably easier task, since this minority kept detailed accounts. From these it is sometimes possible to find out exactly what they bought and how they used it in their meals. This chapter looks at the household accounts from a number of different sources, beginning with a small chantry in Bridport, Dorset.

The two priests who lived at Munden's Chantry in the middle of the fifteenth century were hardly better off than the town or country middle class, but this example serves as an introduction to the lifestyle of the richer classes. Their basic diet was similar to that already described for peasants and townsfolk, including much bread (neither quality nor colour were specified in their accounts), quantities of meat (usually beef, mutton and pork; veal and lamb on occasion; but never bacon, unless 'porcinis' also meant bacon). The meat was bought throughout the year and appears always to have been fresh. Fish was another staple of their diet, and was eaten every week on Wednesdays, Fridays and

Saturdays, as was usual, with meat eaten on the other days. Fish replaced meat completely during Lent. The variety of fish was very wide indeed. Fresh fish included mackerel, hake, haddock, herrings and conger eel. These were bought as needed. Salt fish included ling, hake, cod and whiting. Some of these, particularly the whiting, may have been salted at home using some of the large amount of coarse salt that was bought. Some manors kept huge stocks of salt. In the thirteenth century the Bishop of Winchester kept 160 quarters at one of his manors. Much shellfish was eaten, among which were mussels, whelks, cockles and, the favourite, oysters. Eggs, butter, cheese and milk were also bought as they did not keep any cattle. Dairy products seem to have been available at all times of the year. They had a garden containing vines and fruit trees, all of which were regularly pruned, sometimes by the carpenter. The trees must have provided a certain amount of fruit even though they bought crab apples (probably to make verjuice from) and other fresh fruit. None are mentioned in these accounts, but lemons were commonly imported and used in cooking. Fresh vegetables, including quite large quantities of peas and beans, were bought. Some of the peas were for the pigeons they kept (and probably ate). They probably grew other vegetables, certainly onions, since they twice purchased onion seed. The fuel used for cooking and heating was evidently charcoal. Honey was used for sweetening, and a pot costing 8d. apparently lasted a year.

They bought about 5 or 6 gallons of ale per week. They did not apparently brew their own, as was common practice in richer households. The ale was usually of the second class, as perhaps befitted their ecclesiastical status. A better class of ale was purchased for special occasions, such as when they had guests. Wine was apparently drunk only with visitors. They made, and presumably drank, perry (fermented pear juice) and possibly cider, since they bought a perry sieve. If they did not buy much wine they certainly bought other luxuries for special treats. Sometimes sucking pigs or chickens were bought, once the two chaplains had a woodcock each, and one very special occasion they had a goose which cost 6d. During Lent they considerably lightened the rigours of the season by buying figs (in 1454 2 lb cost 1½d.), raisins, dates and almonds. Considerable quantities of almonds were used in cooking, partly in the preparation of 'almond milk' which replaced cow's milk on fast days.[1]

Almonds and raisins were also bought at Christmas, perhaps for a Christmas pudding. Apart from this there is no sign that they celebrated Christmas by eating anything very different from their normal diet. This is presumably not due to their religious status, since this did not inhibit other ecclesiastical establishments. For example, in 1289 Richard de Swinfield, the Bishop of Hereford, spent Christmas at his manor of Prestbury, near Gloucester. The day before Christmas was kept as a fast, but a considerable amount of fish, herrings, conger eels and codlings were eaten, together with a salmon costing 5s. 8d. (28p, quite a high price). A dozen cups, 300 dishes, 150 large plates and 200 small plates were obtained for the occasion. There were a number of guests – at least fifteen judging by the number of extra horses in the stable for the next two days. On the following day (Christmas Day) even more food was consumed. Over three days they ate no less than 1 boar, 2 complete carcasses and 3 quarters of beef, 2 calves, 4 does, 4 pigs, about 60 fowls (hens or possibly capons), 8 partridges and 2 geese, as well as bread and cheese. The amount of ale served was not recorded, but ten sextaries (about 40 gallons) of red wine and one of white were consumed. This is a fairly modest amount for about 70 people. On such occasions the wine was sometimes only served to the bishop and the most important guests. The amount of food was also considerable and (as the editor of the account suggests), probably a large amount was given to the poor, or perhaps to the manor tenants.[2]

Spices, such as ginger, cloves and cinnamon, saffron and mustard were also purchased. They did not need to buy very much pepper since ½ lb of pepper cloves formed part of their original endowment. Spices always formed part of the diet of gentry and magnate households, presumably because they liked the flavour these gave to food. The spices must also have helped to improve the flavour of the very large amounts of dried and salt fish they ate. There is no evidence that medieval people frequently ate food that was tainted or decaying, in fact there is some evidence that they took precautions to avoid this. The spices were thus not primarily to disguise the flavour of bad food. The two priests frequently had visitors to meals, sometimes workers, such as masons, whom they were employing. Nothing special was provided (usually no food is listed), but sometimes food was offered in quite large quantities. On one occasion in January 1455 there were six guests – local worthies including the Rector of Bridport and the Prior of St John's. Much food was bought that week, including a sucking pig, a goose, two cocks, eggs, raisins and the best ale. The total spent was 2s. 3½d., while the weekly expenses of the Chantry household were, on average, less than 5s. To this was added a payment of 5d. to 'Willelmo Baker' for making pies and for flour that he had bought.[3]

It has been calculated that 80 per cent of the budget of Munden's Chantry went on food, with another 7.5 per cent on fuel and light. This reflects the fact that the priests' income was relatively low, and indicates that their diet was probably not that different from that of the richer peasants. Their food was, however, certainly varied, interesting and nutritious. This household was at the lower end of the gentry scale. A wealthier household was that of Dame Alice de Bryene of Acton Hall, Suffolk, for whom a household book of

1412–13 exists.[4] This household was larger than Munden's Chantry and was more typical of gentry households, buying much food on a large scale to keep in stock and use as needed. The chantry only stored food on a very small scale. Dame Alice's household also brewed its own ale and baked its own bread, which the Chantry priests did not.[5]

The Bryene accounts give much detail. Daily purchases (both for stock and for immediate use) and the issue of store items were listed. The amount of malt used in brewing ale and the amount of ale drunk each day were also set down. A complete picture of what was bought and what happened to it was thus provided. The similarities and differences between this household and the smaller one in Bridport are interesting. The similarities lie in the diet. Beef, pork, lamb and bacon were purchased, much bread was eaten (white and 'black'; see below) and fish, both fresh and salt, were included in the diet. The purchase of bacon is not unexpected (it was unusual that the priests of the chantry never bought it). The fresh fish were mostly cod, mackerel, plaice, sole, merlings (whiting) and skate (thornbacks), although others, such as garfish, salmon and sturgeon, were also bought. Eels, dace and other kinds of fresh-water fish were not mentioned. These may have been obtained from manor resources and so would not have appeared in these accounts. The Earl of Northumberland's household was certainly provided with fresh fish from one of his manors in 1512. The herrings in the Bryene household seem never to have been fresh, but were recorded as white, salted (pickled in brine), red, or salted and smoked. Other salt fish – eels, 'lyngs' and 'chelyngges' – were also bought.[6] The latter two were dried cod of various species. Stockfish (usually also dried members of the cod family only very much harder) were also bought. These were so hard that a special hammer was needed to deal with them. As the Goodman of Paris said, 'when it hath been kept a long time and it is desired to eat it, it behoves to beat it with a wooden hammer for a full hour, and then set it to soak in warm water for a full two hours or more'. Even then it was better to eat it soaked in butter. Oysters (from Colchester), 'muxlys' (mussels), 'welkes' and 'schrympys' were also eaten.[7]

Milk and cream were bought in the summer but not at other times. During other seasons these were probably supplied from animals on the estates. Butter and cheese were apparently bought throughout the year. The household bought one wey of cheese (a Suffolk wey was, later at least, 256 lb) from the farmer of 'the lady's manor' in the autumn.[8] There is no reference to the preservation of these dairy products by salting, but this must have been carried out occasionally. Fresh butter must have been in very short supply at some times in the year. Butter and cheese were very heavily salted in the Middle Ages. For example, in 1305 the Bishop of Worcester used 1 lb of salt for every 10 lb of butter or cheese. Most of the eggs appear to have been bought, in small numbers and from somewhere other than farm chickens. The young chickens received as gifts were either eaten quickly or converted into capons and eaten later. Eggs were not often used to accompany fish, as was frequently the case in other households. Eggs on their own or used in cooking were not eaten during Lent as this was strictly forbidden. It was not forbidden to eat eggs on ordinary fast days. All items were used in larger numbers than in Bridport, and this is where the greatest difference lies. Dame Alice's household entertained far more. There were few days when there was not someone extra to a meal – the household frequently fed 50 in a day, sometimes over 100, and never less than 26, so supplies were neccessarily bought in large quantities.

The goods purchased or obtained from store were listed every day, while the total amount eaten and total expenditure were listed monthly. This information was then summarized in the steward's account at the end of the year. Something that these accounts highlight is the extent to which such a household was self-sufficient. While a great deal of food was purchased, even more was grown on the estates or prepared in the kitchens. All of the very large quantity of grain – wheat, oats, barley, etc. – was grown on the estate. Some of the meat was from animals bred on the estate farms while some was bought in as carcasses. A considerable amount of mutton and a rather smaller amount of lamb was eaten in the Bryene household, as well as a solitary boar. The latter was not eaten at Christmas as might be expected. A large number of sucking pigs were bought, but whether live or as carcasses is not clear. These were on the menu at least once a week and frequently more often. Animals were butchered on the estate throughout the year. The dates in 1419 on which fourteen cows and three steers were killed are given. These reinforce the modern view that animals were not all killed and salted down at Martinmas (11 November).[9] The number killed depended on the amount of fodder likely to be available to feed the survivors and the size of the household. A larger household would have needed more meat to feed the inhabitants, so the necessary slaughter would have been greater. To feed the household of Richard de Swinfield in 1289 (some forty people), 52 cows were bought or brought from the bishop's manors, and some sheep and 22 pigs were obtained from the estates. To these were added an unspecified number of deer caught in the chase and killed on the bishop's various deer parks. The slaughtermen who dealt with all these animals were paid the moderately generous sum of 2s. 6d. (25p), and the salt was bought in Worcester. For a large part of the year fresh meat, as well as salt, would have been available.[10]

Two of the cows on the Bryene Estate were not slaughtered in 1419 because they had disappeared. One was stolen that July and the other went astray at about the same time. Obviously they did not know the precise date. The stray was never found, despite due 'proclamation made for the same'. The hides of the animals that were killed were either sold or were used in the household. The tallow was also used in the household. The rabbits eaten were all caught on the estates and their skins 'delivered to the Lady' for use. Staff such as the cook or the laundress were, in small households, often called on to prepare such skins for use. Such economies (using animal by-products to produce items that would otherwise have to be bought) were common. Most of the chickens, capons, pigeons, pheasants and partridges eaten came from the farms, although a lot of capons were received as gifts. Not all of these were eaten, a note in the steward's account notes that in 1419, thirty-nine 'strayed away and were destroyed but how is not known'.[11] This note was deleted in the account after it was written, perhaps to avoid questions being asked.

One type of food that could not be grown on the estate was spice. The volume and variety bought were much more in line with those of the gentry or noble households than were the similar purchases of the Munden Chantry priests. No less than 3 lb of pepper were bought in 1419, together with smaller amounts of ginger, cinnamon, saffron, cloves and mace. Also included under the heading 'Spice' were 10 lb of raisins ('Reysynes de Corynes', that is raisins of Corinth), dates, 40 lb of almonds, 4 lb of figs and 1 lb of white sugar. 'Spices' thus included much that we would not class as such. The amount spent on these goods was 54s. 10d. (£2.74), rather more than was spent on average each month for all food in 1412–13. Most of the spice buying was carried out by the 'lady'. The amount of spices bought by bigger households was sometimes very large. For example, in 1452–3 the Duke of Buckingham bought no less than 316 lb of pepper and 194 lb of ginger. He also bought a greater variety of items. For instance among others he bought 'blaunchpoudre' (ginger ground with sugar); and 'alkanet', 'turnsole' and 'saundrez', which were dyes (red, purple and red, respectively) used in food. The purchases of spices in the Bryene household in 1412–13 were very similar to those described above, except for there being much more sugar (56 lb which cost 9½d.) and 13 pints of honey (which cost 26d.). The lack of honey purchases in 1419 may indicate that most of the household's needs were obtained from home hives. Still included at this time with the spices was rice, of which the household used about 4 lb a year. It was much used in Lent as a whitening and thickening agent, and sometimes as flour.

Very few vegetables were mentioned in the accounts, except sometimes onions and garlic, and one quarter and one bushel of green peas in 1419. The latter were made into pottage for Dame Alice and her household servants. Grey peas were bought and made into bread (possibly for horses), and also given to the domestic pigeons. The onions and garlic were used in large amounts as flavourings, as were mustard and vinegar. Vegetables are mentioned in the household accounts of Richard de Swinfield in 1290. These include the usual onions and leeks, peas and beans, and once some kind of salted or pickled greens. For the amount of vegetables eaten see Chapter 4.[12]

All of the bread used by Dame Alice's household was baked on the premises. Baking occurred once a week (about average for this kind of household) using a quarter (400 lb) of wheat. Most of the loaves were white, and presumably of good quality, although this is not stated. A much smaller number were 'black'. Their quality is in doubt, though they were certainly brown wheat bread (not black rye bread) since it was always made from the same wheat as the white bread. The proportion made was usually about 240 white to about 30 brown ones from a quarter of wheat. The actual numbers depended on the quality of the grain. The loaves were of the usual size (about 2 lb), and from the proportions the 'white' loaves cannot have been of the very best quality. Making this quality entailed removing a large part of the bran (for the very finest up to about one-third as opposed to this household's one bushel per quarter, an extraction rate of one-eighth). A small amount of bread was made from pea flour. Dame Alice appears not to have made bread from maslin (rye and wheat) or any of the other mixed grains, as did many households for trencher bread or for the servants. The 'black' loaves were probably eaten by the lower servants, but many of the staff must have eaten the white bread. The 'black' loaves were presumably made from the sieved flour with the addition of bran, while the white loaves were made from the sieved flour alone.[13]

The household brewed all of the ale it drank about once a week. It was always made from 2 quarters of malt, of which 1 quarter was drage malt (made from mixed oats and barley rather than pure barley). This made 112 gallons of ale. Since the number of mealtime guests during the week would have been about 220, then (allowing for the servants) each guest would apparently have been expected to drink about a gallon of ale a day. This is not an unusual allowance. The ale was rather weaker than that usually brewed elsewhere. In other households not more than 90 gallons were made from this quantity of barley, and a more usual amount was between 50 and 75 gallons. In 1512 the Earl of Northumberland had 96 gallons brewed from two quarters of malt, and 88 in the summer when it had to be made 'bigger' to prevent 'turnynge', although this was hopped beer. Ale would not keep, so each batch had to be drunk by the time another was made. The other mealtime drink was wine. 'Wine from supply' always appeared on the list of victuals in the Bryene household. Whether it was given to all visitors or only to those of high rank is not specified. It was usual to give ale to lesser knights and those of lower rank, albeit of the best quality. Similarly in the Abbey at Ramsay in 1284, each monk was given given ½ gallon of wine on festival days only (and on the feast day of the abbot), whereas visitors and the abbey dignitaries had wine every day. Judging from the amount bought by the Bryene household, wine was probably not given to all visitors. Thus in the account for 1419, two pipes and one hogshead of red wine, one hogshead of white wine (i.e. 262 gallons of red and 105 gallons of white), two small barrels of sweet wine, one of 'Rumneye' and the other of 'Malmesyn', and a separate quart of white wine 'for the lady' (of a superior quality) were purchased. The better quality white wine cost 2d., that is 8d. per gallon, the price of a good wine at this time. Poorer wine cost 3d. or 4d. per gallon, although the Earl of Northumberland expected to pay an average of just over 5d. per gallon for his 2,184 gallons in 1512. The lower quality red and white wine bought for Lady Bryene cost a total of just over £13 (including carriage). Buying in bulk in this way saved money. All of the wine for the Bryene household was bought in London or Ipswich by the mistress of the household. The empty barrels, including those that had contained salt fish, were thriftily sold when empty.[14]

These accounts are also interesting in that they show the changes in consumption that occurred in Lent, at harvest and during ploughing. In Lent the number of herrings eaten rose by about 50 per cent, and more fresh fish and shellfish (mussels, whelks and oysters) were purchased. The household continued to have the usual three meals a day, although strictly speaking only one should have been eaten in Lent. The monks of Winchester did the same. The Bryene household did abstain from eggs as was expected of them. The monks of Winchester ate figs and raisins to soften the rigours of their diet, as did the residents of Munden's chantry (see above). There is no record of whether the Bryene household did so, or whether they bought olive oil for frying in Lent when animal products were forbidden. No less than 36 gallons of olive oil (at a cost of 33s. 3d., £1.66) were purchased by the Earl of Northumberland in 1512. There is no record that either household ate barnacle geese in Lent. These were believed by some to develop from barnacles (or a worm of some kind) and to live only in the sea, and could therefore be classed as fish by some and eaten in Lent with a clear conscience. This was expressly opposed by the Church, but some still ate the geese on fast days. The same applied to the tail of the beaver. On the three days before Ash Wednesday no fish at all was eaten, but a great deal more meat than usual. Otherwise the Bryene household normally adhered strictly to the pattern of meat on Sunday to Tuesday and Thursday, with fish on the other days. Much more meat than usual was eaten on Easter Sunday too, including no less than twenty pigeons, and unusually, some veal. The rather grander household of Richard de Swinfield, Bishop of Hereford in the late fourteenth century, also ate considerable quantities of meat at Easter 1289. In this case they consumed 208 pigeons, 'three fat deer', 1400 eggs and large numbers of capons, kids and beef.[15]

The spring ploughing on the Bryene Estate in 1413 was in late April rather than during Lent. For the three days that it seems to have lasted the number of guests rose considerably, but the only obvious change in food consumption was an increase in the amount of bread eaten on one of the days, despite the added presence of ten of the manor household together with the bailiff and twelve 'strange ploughmen'. This was not the case during the summer harvest which went on for most of August, when the increase in consumption was dramatic. The amount of ale brewed doubled to over 1,000 gallons with brewing taking place twice a week, and the number of loaves baked also rose. Four times there were special bakings for the 'boon workers' (up to 92 workers on one day), each time making fewer loaves (just over a hundred). All of them were apparently 'white', and usually made from a quarter of wheat. The weight of each loaf would therefore have been about 4 lb (twice the normal size). There were corresponding increases in the amount of food used in general, including an increase in the consumption of meat. The boon workers, or at least some of them, appear to have been fed for all meals, not only in the evening. Another unusual event was the meal for 300 tenants on the first day of the year in 1413, which happened to be a Sunday. No less than 314 white loaves and 40 black loaves were issued from the pantry on that day, and among other items were 2 pigs (another 5 pigs were bought), 12 geese, 24 capons and 17 rabbits from the kitchen. Seventeen gallons of milk were bought for the occasion and ale was also issued.[16]

These two households (that of the two priests at Munden's Chantry and of Dame Alice de Bryene) have been discussed in detail since they show more easily how the households operated than larger, richer ones do. Farther up the social scale there are naturally more accounts, some of which record lavish feasts. These will be described later as they are hardly typical of the everyday life of the upper aristocracy and of the royal family who lived surprisingly frugally. The basic diet varied very little from one end of the gentry spectrum to the other, and always consisted of bread (albeit the best white), meat or fish, and ale. Care was taken to buy meat when it was at its cheapest, and damaged goods were used if possible. Thus in the Earl of Northumberland's household in 1512, 'brokyn' (sour) wines were ordered to be made into vinegar, and the bran that was left over when wheat was milled for white bread was made into bread for use as trenchers. The bran was mixed with some flour, since it would not make bread on its own (see below). Sometimes in other households, bread baked from 'maslin' was used to make trenchers. All bread and beer were made in the household itself. How much was involved is unknown, but it was perhaps not as much as the

40,000 or so gallons of ale that the Duke of Buckingham used in 1452–3.[17]

The very much larger quantity of food involved was of course one of the differences between these households and lesser ones. One of the other differences was the more exotic foods bought: porpoise and many kinds of birds such as seagulls, woodcocks, 'wypes' (lapwings), thrushes and larks were all served only to the lord, in this case the Earl of Northumberland. He apparently did not eat puffins, which must have been very oily (they, like barnacle geese, were classified as fish; see above). A certain amount of game was included in the diet too. The rabbits eaten in quite humble households were, in a sense, game, since after the early Norman period rabbits were rarely obtained from kept warrens but were caught from the wild. It is difficult to assess the actual contribution of game to the diet of the aristocratic household because, since it was neither bought nor sold, it was not always recorded in the accounts. It was listed in the household book of the Earl of Northumberland, however. In 1512 he expected to take a total of 49 deer (29 does and 20 bucks) from his parks for use in his household.[18] This was not a very large part of the meat expected to be eaten in that year, which consisted of 123 cows, 667 sheep, 25 pigs, 28 veal calves, 60 lambs, and rabbits and birds of various kinds. The Earl of Oxford and his household ate only 36 deer in 1431–2, but this was a larger percentage of their total consumption of meat. Game, which included the more prestigious types of fresh-water fish (bream and pike), was served at the table of the lord or lady on special occasions or to special guests. Many of these, and sometimes lesser, fish were obtained in noble (and religious) households from the stew (storage) ponds. Birds caught when hawking, a passion of the higher ranks, were another source of game. The amount that this added to the table was probably negligible.

From the household accounts it is possible to get some idea

of the amount eaten at particular meals. Thus the Earl of
Northumberland and his countess at breakfast, on a day on
which meat was eaten, were given a manchet loaf (that is a 2
lb loaf of best quality) each and one loaf of bread in
trenchers. In the Northumberland household trencher bread,
thick slices of which were used to eat from, was made from
the coarse meal that came from the mill after the removal of
the best flour. This would have been of poorer quality than
the trencher bread made from maslin, which was used in the
le Strange household in Hunstanton, Norfolk, in 1428. The
loaves of trencher bread were larger than those for household
bread, at least in the Northumberland household. In addition
to bread the Earl and his wife received a quart of beer, a
quart of wine, half a 'chine' of mutton or a chine of boiled
beef (the exact size of a 'chine' of meat varied with the type
of meat but would hardly have been less than 2–3 lb). On
fish days, in place of the meat, they had a dish of butter with
a piece of salt fish, or a 'Dysch of Butter'd Eggs'.[19] Other
members of the household received similar meals, but in
smaller amounts, lacking the wine and with the bread
changing to household bread rather than manchet. This
latter change came with those of the status of 'my Ladys
Gentylwomen' who also sometimes received 'three muton
Bonys boyled' rather than a piece of meat.

Some of the servants who waited on the earl, the countess
and their family or the chief household officers were not
always given a regular issue of food but received the
'revercion' of the food given to the others. Thus the two sons
of the earl were served by five people at supper in the
'scambling' days of Lent (when informal meals were served),
and these five were to eat the reversion (that is what was left
after the two boys had eaten). Since it appears that most of
the bread and drink would have been consumed, they were
given two loaves of bread and two gallons of beer to go with
the remnants. Similar arrangements applied in the

household of Henry VIII in 1526, and apparently not only in Lent. No extra bread and beer seem to have been allowed to those having the reversion, and the 'reversion of the residue of messes of meate served to the Queen's Chamber' was given to the almoner.[20]

Most of the lower orders in the Northumberland household who were given their meals received bread, beer and meat or fish, but at the bottom of the scale, in the porter's lodge and stable, they received only bread and beer. At least the bread appears to have been 'household' bread and not that made from mixed corn, rye, barley and beans which servants were given at Bolton Priory. This distinction between social levels was common, and is evident in cases where a household account covers a period when the lord was absent from home. For example, in 1337, when the Bishop of Bath and Wells was absent from home, fresh meat and other luxuries disappeared from the record and were entirely replaced by bread, ale, bacon and mutton for the staff who remained behind. The cost of feeding each level of a household was occasionally set down. In one instance it ranged from the lord at 7d. per day, through 4d. for an esquire and 3d. for a yeoman, to 1d. for a groom. The enormous amount of food consumed in a large household is shown by calculations made by Maurice Keen for that of the Earl of Northumberland. According to Keen's figures, in one year the household used nearly 17,000 bushels of wheat, 27,500 gallons of ale, 1,600 gallons of wine, nearly 21,000 lb of currants, 124 beef cattle, 667 sheep and 14,000 herrings. When divided by the number of people that had to be fed, these quantities are not that large. Thus each person received an average of about 1½ quarts of ale per day. The procurement of such large amounts of goods would have taken a considerable amount of planning to ensure that all was bought and ready when needed.[21]

Attempts have been made to estimate the amount of income spent on food. Not unexpectedly the proportion spent fell as income rose. The chantry at Bridport spent more than half of its income on food, while a rich knight, Sir Hugh Luttrell of Dunster in the 1420s spent rather less than half. Rich earls expected to spend less than one quarter of their income on food. There were exceptions to this rule. For example in 1345–6, Sir Thomas Berkeley of Berkeley spent 57 per cent of his income on food and some monasteries spent more than two thirds of theirs. Smaller households spent more on bread and ale, while magnates spent a greater proportion on wine and spices.[22] Some of these variations undoubtedly reflected the advantages gained through bulk buying, or the fact that larger amounts of food came from the estates of magnates.

FIVE

ADULTERATION AND NUTRITION

The quality of food in the Middle Ages, in the sense of its purity, is difficult to determine. It must have been very variable, much more so than at present, since there were no really effective quality control measures in operation. Producers would send to market whatever they had grown or made and it was up to the consumer to take care in what he bought. There was also the problem of the deliberate adulteration of goods: the selling of goods low in quality and deliberately short in weight. Measures were taken against at least some of these problems, and both the town authorities and central government tried to ensure that the food was 'of the nature and quality demanded.[1] These efforts were restricted very largely, but not entirely, to food staples, that is bread, ale, meat and fish. Most important was that, as far as possible, the goods were of a standard weight and price. As already described, as early as 1266 (repeating a much earlier Act), the *Assisa Panis et Cervisiae* ruled that the price and weight of various types of loaf should be related to the price of corn (and the same applied to ale). This assize of bread was repeated both nationally and locally at intervals throughout the Middle Ages.[2] The original Act allowed for bread of several different qualities: 'bread of the better, second or third sort'. This was regularly repeated in subsequent Acts and local ordinances for the selling of ale, wine and various other goods. Such ruling usually also fixed the retail price of, for example, a gallon of Gascon, 'Rhenish' or the sweet 'Malvesey' wine. In the sixteenth century an attempt was made to regulate similarly the wholesale price of wine, but this was not wholly successful.[3]

Weights and measures were standardized as far as practicable, but even so the state of affairs was fairly chaotic. A concern with weights and measures was the other side of a regard for quality. The *Assisa Panis* attempted to dictate the size of weights and measures. This was repeated at intervals, notably in the statutes of Edward III, under Henry VI and Richard III. The latter's Act, the Contents of Vessels of Wine and Oil, was re-enacted several times in the sixteenth century. These acts laid down the sizes of the tun, hogshead, etc., in which wine was allowed to be imported. It was important that the King's officers, particularly the wine gaugers (who measured the amount of wine in a barrel before it could be sold), were confident that they were dealing with standard-sized barrels. The 'non-standard' foreign wine barrels caused endless problems. Retail weights and measures were also very firmly regulated. Taverners in London, for example, were ordered to sell their wine in standard measures, which had been certified as true by the sheriff, never by the 'gruskyn' (the small cup from which the wine was drunk). The same applied to ale which could only legally be sold by the gallon, the pottle (½ gallon) or the quart, all of which were strictly defined measures. These had to be assayed and marked as accurate by the alderman of the ward. Anyone found selling wine or ale by anything other than correctly 'sealed' measures could be fined and sent to prison.[4]

In general it was the duty of the town guilds to maintain the purity of the goods that they sold, and in the main they do seem to have tried to do so. They were helped in this by the government of the town. Much is known of London in this respect, and the City records give an interesting picture of the quality of the food sold in the markets and shops. For example, there are many cases in the published City of London letter books of the punishment of bakers for selling lightweight bread, and there are several instances where bread was found to contain bad dough. 'Foreign' bakers were sometimes accused of selling bread made of bad paste. In a case in 1311. For example a baker was found guilty of selling putrid bread made from putrid wheat.[5] In 1419 it was ruled that no loaf should be coated with bran. This was presumably to avoid falsifying the weight, not because of a prejudice against bran. Cases of actual adulteration, involving the deliberate addition of inferior (and cheaper) materials, are rare. Bread was in one instance found to contain sand, and in 1311 bad dough was contained within a casing of good dough. Other cases involved a baker who was found guilty of making bread of dirt and 'coppewebbes', and another who made a loaf with dirt and ashes. In this latter case it seems likely that the loaf was merely contaminated with ashes from the oven fire. The case of the baker's assistant found guilty of adding a piece of iron to a loaf was not a deliberate attempt to adulterate the bread but a panic attempt to conceal a low-weight loaf from the mayor and alderman when on an assize of bread tour. One real attempt at adulteration occurred in York in 1589, when three bakers were found guilty of selling ground meal to the poor which was composed (apparently regularly) of bad corn, rye, barley, beans and oats, mixed with bran, 'chesell' (probably small sand or gravel) and other similar materials.[6]

Another regulation stated that no one was allowed to mix bad corn with good, similar to another (repeated several times) against mixing good wine with bad. The latter must have been very tempting since the customer would not have noticed it and it would have disposed of bad wine. Practices such as this must have been one of the reasons for the ruling that the customer had to be able to see into the cellar to view from which barrel wine was being drawn, and also to ensure that customers could see that the vessel into which the wine was drawn was clean. Keepers of hostelries were known to hang a curtain over the cellar doorway to obscure this view.[7] That regulations against nefarious practices were very necessary is clear from many references in the City of London Letter Books. These show that, despite overseeing by the Vintners' Company whose searchers were supposed to check on the presence of bad wines in taverns (and presumably did so as far as possible), cases still occurred of taverners accused of selling unsound red wine, 'unwholesome for man, in deceit of the common people . . . and to the shameful disgrace of the officers of the City'. The taverner in this case, one John Penrose, was found guilty, condemned to drink a draught of the wine 'which he sold to the common people', and the remainder of the wine was to be poured over his head. He was also forbidden from following the vintners' trade in the City of London 'for ever', although he was readmitted to the trade five years later.[8] There is no explanation of how the wine in this case was unsound (it was presumably sour), but there is no doubt what was wrong in some later cases.

In 1419 a proclamation was issued by the City against the counterfeiting of 'Romeney' wine (a sweet wine from Greece) by the addition to 'wyne of Spayne, Rochell, and other remenauntz of brokyn, sodyn, reboyllid and other unthrifty wynes of other contrees' of pitch, wax and 'other horrible and unholsome things' to restore the colour and make them look and taste like 'Romeney' wine. However these additions affected the colour it seems unlikely that they did much for the flavour. According to the proclamation there was apparently a great deal of this counterfeit wine about in the City, as well as mixed wine (good with bad and one type with another). Selling one type of wine as another seems to have been fairly common, although it was illegal. All of these practices were forbidden 'that no man withyn this Citee ne the liberte therof, fre ne forein, coloure ne medle no manere wyn, that is to sey no white with rede, old with newe, hole with brokyn or corrupt, rochel with renyssh, ne othere wyne of divers kyndes ne growynges to gidir' under the penalty of the confiscation of the wine and standing in the pillory for the culprit. That this did not stop the practice is clear from a case that immediately followed the proclamation of 1419 in the City of London Letter Books. William Horold, a cooper, was convicted of adding to his 'old and feble Spaynissh wyn' gums and other 'unholsome' things as well as powdered bay and other powders to restore the colour. The gum would have added to the body of a thin wine, while sugar, if added, would have improved the flavour.[9]

It is also possible that not only was 'new' wine concocted by the methods described above, but that wine was actually made by the simple expedient of mixing spices with 'burning water' (alcohol). These techniques were described in a sixteenth-century book, *Treasure of Euonymous*, published in 1559. The spices used to make 'Rhenish' were cinnamon, ginger and cloves, and these were steeped in alcohol for 12 hours. No water was added so that the resulting 'wine' was either very strong or the alcohol very weak. Since these instructions existed it seems fairly certain that they were used, although the 'wine' produced cannot have fooled many people. In some ways it is difficult to understand quite what would have been considered bad wine, in view of the habit of drinking it from casks that had been open for many weeks (see p. 53).[10]

To try to inhibit adulteration and the mixing of wines, it was forbidden to keep wine from Gascony, Rochelle and Spain in the same cellar as Rhenish wine. This must have been very difficult for a taverner to achieve, even if he wished to. The prohibition against selling Gascon wine and wine from other countries in the same tavern was also intended to help keep the sale of the latter outside the control of the Vintners Company who, up to 1530, had a monopoly on the sale of Gascon wines in the City of London, but not on the other wines. Licences for the sale of sweet wines and 'Rhenish' were granted separately. In 1594 the vintners were accused of adding such items as alum, turnsole (a purple dye), starch and aromatics, so these practices obviously continued.[11] To keep them in check, 'searchers' were appointed every year. Their duty was to check the condition of wines in all taverns in the City of London, and to condemn and destroy it if necessary, as it frequently was. Even so not all bad wine was discovered, and fraud was probably common. During the reign of Edward IV, one priest in the City was sold wine guaranteed to be as good Gascon wine as any in London. However, he said (when prosecuting the seller in the court of Chancery) that it was three parts false and consisted of the corrupt and decolorized dregs of more than 100 tuns.[12]

Ale, the other alcoholic drink on regular sale, was also often adulterated, and it was not unknown for bad ale to be sold. In 1377 it was decided in London (and later in other towns) to appoint 'Alkonneres'. These officials were appointed at intervals. They had to take an oath to be ready to taste ale at any time they were informed that a new brew was ready (by the raising of an ale stake by the brewer); to check that it was up to the proper quality and, if not good enough to sell at the assize price, to set a price. Ale was supposed to be witheld from sale until it had been checked in this manner, under pain of forfeiture. These attempts seem, in general, to have gone a long way towards maintaining the quality of this staple drink.[13] It did not, needless to say, stop all attempts to cheat the public. There are many local records of poor ale being sold, and of the brewers being punished for selling it. Sometimes very large numbers were involved – nearly ninety in one day on occasion, although some of these would have been selling above the assize price as well as selling ale of poor quality. Ale must have gone off and become unwholesome very quickly as a result of bacterial action, especially in the summer. There was little that could be done about this. Lacking any knowledge of the cause it was not strictly the fault of the brewer, but the aleconners would still take note of it.

Ale was probably frequently adulterated by the addition of water. This would have been very difficult to detect if done in moderation by the methods then available. Salt and resin were also frequently added. Ale must very frequently have been sold by short measure, too. One particularly blatant case was in London in 1364, when Alice de Caustone was found guilty of selling ale in a quart pot that was not only not sealed (as a sign that it was a true measure), but contained in the bottom 1½ inches of pitch, on top of which was rosemary to conceal it. The vessel actually held less than three quarters of a quart.[14] The iniquities of the ale wife were well known in the Middle Ages. In the Chester Mystery Plays the woman 'taverner' in hell laments her use of untrue measures and of hops (see below). The ale wife Eleanor Rummyng, written about in 1517, did more than use inaccurate measures. She allowed her hens to roost over the fermenting vessel, 'And somtymes she blennes The donge of her hennes And the ale togyder', which made the ale brew quicker and also improved the complexion. This was described in a poem by John Skelton. This story may have been slightly exaggerated, but such adulteration was probably well known. This particular practice must have given an interesting flavour to the ale.

Most of the ale sold was brewed by individuals, mostly women, working on a very small scale. This altered with the introduction of beer since this was more easily brewed on a large scale. In some cases, as in Havering, Essex, the change occurred very quickly. Here in 1464–5 all of the 21 brewers and ale sellers were female, but by the end of the century there was only one woman out of 15.[15] It had been common to brew ale with added herbs to give interesting flavours, but beer (that is ale brewed with hops; see Chapter 1) was not made in England until about the fifteenth century. However, beer was known in England from almost as soon as it was brewed on a large scale on the Continent in the thirteenth century. In 1289 a Norwich ale seller was charged with selling 'Flanders beer' contrary to the assize of ale. The first mention in the London records appears to be in 1391. In that year there was a reference to 'hoppyngbeer' in the City of London Letter Books. Beer had obviously been imported for many years and seems by the beginning of the fifteenth century, in the south of England at least, to have been accepted without much opposition. The 1391 reference contains no comment since it is merely a price regulation. London sent both ale and beer to Henry V in France in 1418. More beer was sent than ale (300 tuns of the former but only 200 of the latter), but the beer was valued at less than the ale at 13s. 4d. (66p) to the tun compared with 30s. (£1.50).[16] It is apparent that there were mixed feelings in England about the use of hops, and they were for some time regarded (by some, at least) as an adulteration of good English ale. For example, in about 1426 a brewer was accused of putting an unwholesome weed known as a 'hopp' into his ale.

In 1436 'malevolent attempts' were being made in England to stop natives of Holland and Zealand from brewing and selling beer on the grounds that it 'was poisonous and not fit to drink', and also caused drunkenness. Henry VI issued a proclamation saying that, on the contrary, it was a wholesome drink, especially in the summer, and that attacks on brewers, preventing them from carrying on their trade, must be stopped. Soon after this, in 1441, Henry appointed two surveyors of 'berebrewers' to operate in much the same way as did the aleconnors, checking that all materials used were sound, and especially that 'les hoppes' were not too dry or rotten, and that the grain used did not contain the worms called 'wifles'. The beer had to be surveyed eight days after brewing, unlike ale which was surveyed almost immediately.[17] By 1464 the 'mistery of berebruers' felt sufficiently established to petition the Mayor and Aldermen of the City of London for regulations governing their craft, as did all the other trades and crafts of the City. This was duly granted to them and they were officially recognized as a guild in 1493.

Despite this official recognition there was still some antagonism towards the use of hops in England, and fulminations against their use continued. In 1484 the (Ale) Brewers Guild in London petitioned that no one should be allowed to put anything in ale but malt and yeast (and certainly not hops). As late as 1512 the authorities in Shrewsbury forbade the use of hops, 'that wicked and pernicious weed'. Andrew Borde, in 1542, believed that pure ale, containing nothing except malt, water and yeast, was the natural drink for the Englishman and made him strong. Beer, however, was the natural drink for the Dutchman, and made a man fat and inflated the belly. It was not considered entirely bad, though, since it 'qualified' the heat of the liver if well made, even if it did kill those who 'be troubled with the colycke'. A slightly ambiguous reference in the 1526 Eltham Ordinances of Henry VIII forbade Henry's brewer to put hops or brimstone into his ale, but this is in addition to the provision of beer, so it appears that Henry wanted to have pure ale and was not forbidding the brewing of beer. Beer steadily gained acceptance, aided by the fact that it was generally cheaper to produce than ale since more beer could be made from a given amount of malt. This was an important consideration in the later sixteenth century, a period of inflation. By the beginning of the next century, hops had been accepted to the extent that, in 1604, an Act of James I fulminated against the practice of importing and using hops mixed with dirt, leaves and many other substances to the detriment of the health of the King's subjects. The use of hops was in fact an important advance in the improvement of quality, since they contain natural preservatives which prevented the brew from going off quickly, as ale did. Hops also changed the character of the beverage, from a fairly sweet drink, with the sweetness balanced by natural lactic acid produced by micro-organisms in the yeast, to a more bitter drink caused by the bitterness of the hops.[18]

So far as other foodstuffs were concerned, attempts were made to prevent the sale of bad meat and fish. For example, butchers were forbidden to sell their meat by candlelight. The sale of 'contagious flesh or that died of the murren' was not allowed, although this did not prevent some of the more extreme attempts to defraud the public. For example, one man found a dead pig in the City of London ditch and sold the meat from it, both cooked and raw. One of his customers, Agnes le Ismongere (that is Ironmonger, probably the daughter or wife of an ironmonger), was accused of selling this apparently 'putrid and stinking meat' 'to the peril of the lives of persons buying the same'. She was acquitted, but the finder of the pig was condemned to the pillory and the meat was burned beneath him – the usual penalty. If the meat was as bad as was said, it is difficult to see how Agnes could have been as innocent as she made out, and how anyone could have bought the meat. Cooked meat was sold by the cooks from their own shops (see Chapter 3). They do not always seem to have been very careful with the food that they sold, since one of their ordinances (granted in 1495) laid down that their wardens should have power to oversee 'all manner of dressed victuals in open shops to see if they be wholesome' and, further (in 1475), that no one of the craft 'bake rost nor seeth Flessh nor Fisshe ij tymes to sell'. This was a very wise rule against reheating cooked food, which Chaucer's cook was accused of doing.

It must have been very difficult to detect tainted food in such products as sausages, unless it was very bad, given the widespread and heavy use of spices in meat dishes. This practice may have been partly aimed at legitimately concealing the inevitable natural slow decomposition that occurred in summer. Cases are recorded of butchers puffing air into meat to make the meat look larger, and of stuffing the veins in kidneys with rags to make them weigh more, each presumably a very easily detected fraud. The sale of putrid fish was also known. For example, in 1382 a whole shipload of 7,000 herring and 800 mackerel were sold. Likewise 37 pigeons that were described as 'putrid, rotten, stinking, and abominable to the human race' were put up for sale. Traders were subject to many regulations intended to prevent them from selling decomposing food. Unsalted fish was not allowed to be put on sale for more than two days, and watering fish to freshen it was allowed only twice, although it would have been difficult to detect if this had been done more often.[19] It was certainly understood that eating the flesh of diseased animals was unwise. The statutes of the Sherburn leper hospital in Durham forbade it, although in another similar hospital in Southampton an ox was killed for consumption 'because it was nearly dead'. A certain amount of food poisoning must have been caused by eating such diseased meat, rotten meat and grain.[20]

These instances of attempts to defraud the public are not strictly cases of adulteration, as were, for example, the cases of mixing and colouring wines, but many genuine cases occurred in the grocery trade. Grocery products lend themselves to being combined with other materials, and the Grocers Company of London was well aware of this. By at least the end of the fourteenth century, officials, called 'garblers', were charged with examining imported spices (which could include dried fruit) and similar substances. They were responsible for cleaning it, usually by sieving, to remove dirt, leaves and so on. Groceries could not be sold until they had been garbled. Such was the importance that the company gave to this office that, when it received its charter in 1429, the office of garbler was vested in the warden.[21] It is difficult to see how the garblers carried out their duties successfully when faced with, for example, spices adulterated with false colouring, when sieving would hardly have helped. In 1415, however, there was a case where it was apparently possible to detect the false colouring given to different varieties of ginger by rubbing them together in a sack. The detection by the garbler of 'spice' (for example saffron, ginger or cloves) that had been adulterated by wetting, to increase the weight, was probably relatively easy. Mustard may often have been adulterated, by being mixed with wheat flour, pea flour and radish seeds, as it certainly was in later centuries. Salt, sold by the grocers, as it was by many other tradesmen, was also sometimes adulterated, certainly in France and probably in England too. Thus in the early fourteenth century merchants in Angers were known to mix salt with sand or gravel.[22]

Some of those instances described above would obviously have been health hazards. In any case it seems likely that the quality of food available to the average buyer would have been very variable. Most of the ale and some of the wine, for example, would probably have been very thin, and, in the case of the wine, frequently sour and sometimes diluted with water. It seems likely that, despite considerable official efforts to prevent it, there was a large amount of food adulteration. This would have affected the nutritional value of the food to an extent that is impossible to estimate. Allowing for this, however, it is still possible to estimate how well the various levels of society were nourished.

There was no attempt in the Middle Ages to provide a balanced diet in the sense in which it would be understood today, even in those households where there was a possibility of choice. There was instead the application of the doctrine of the 'humours'. The bodily make-up and characteristics of mankind were thought to be determined by the combination in each person of the four elements (earth, air, fire and water), giving each a typical complexion, qualities and humour depending on how the elements were combined. Thus humanity was divided into different groups depending on the different combination of the four 'humours' (blood, phlegm, yellow or green bile and black bile) that each person contained. Someone with a 'sanguine' complexion was thought to have a hot and moist 'quality' and their humour was 'blood'. An excess of another humour might change someone from one complexion to another, for example an excess of 'green bile' turning a sanguine person into a 'choleric' one. Food was regarded as being of similar composition, thus, for example, older men, who were thought to have an excess of phlegm in their make-up, were advised not to eat lamb since it was thought to have a phlegmatic character.

The whole system was quite logical, given the premises on which it was based. Thus light food was supposed to be eaten before heavy, that is such meat as will make the 'belly soluble', before 'grosse meates'. Drinking between meals was to be avoided, as was over-salty meat, which was thought to cause great 'oppressioun to feble stomakis' and cause them great pain. Too great a variety of food was to be avoided, partly on the grounds that eating too many different kinds required a lot of drink which then hindered digestion. Late meals were also to be avoided. If sleep was essential after eating, Andrew Borde, in the sixteenth century, advised that it should be taken leaning against a cupboard or in a chair because 'slepynge after a full stomacke doth ingendre dyverse infyrmyties; it doth hurte the splen, it relaxeth the synewes, it doth ingendre the dropsyes and the gowte and make a man loke evyll coloured'. Eating white pepper avoided 'rheumes' first thing in the morning.

Many foods were regarded as having good or bad qualities. Beans, for example, nourished the body, and non-fermented bread was good for the stomach. Milk was considered extremely healthy. Ale nourished gross humours and increased the flesh, but on the other hand it gave strength. Old (and 'dark') wine was bad for people, drying up and burning the body, and exciting bile. On the other hand, mulled wine was considered to be a relaxant. New wine, particularly sweet white wine, was also good, provided the grapes had grown on land near hills, the latter being very nutritious and driving away ill humours. However, wine was undoubtedly regarded as bad when drunk in excess. Andrew Borde believed that wine was best drunk diluted with water, preferably distilled (that is distilled with herbs or fruit), or plain water boiled and cooled. He believed that water in general was not good for Englishmen and advised drinking spring water, provided that the spring ran from east to west. Standing water was to be avoided, particularly if putrified (very wise advice). Some authorities believed that water was bad for people whenever it was taken, the view being that drunk after hot meat it 'coldith thy stomac and qwenchith and lettith the hete of digestion, to the grevaunce of the body'. If someone had to drink water because he was hot, he was advised to drink as little as possible.[23]

The doctrine of the humours led to some conclusions thought strange today, such as that fruits were bad, owing to their being over-phlegmatic in their composition and only of use to modify fevers. Overindulgence in fruit can cause diarrhoea which would have been reason enough to advise caution in eating it, although it would increase the risk of not having enough vitamin C in the diet. Milk was thought

Ploughing with oxen, fourteenth century.
Luttrell Psalter, British Library Additional Ms. 42130, f.170

Sowing the seed, fourteenth century.
Luttrell Psalter, British Library Additional Ms. 42130, f.170v

Harvesting with small hand scythes, fourteenth century.
Luttrell Psalter, British Library Additional Ms. 42130, f.172v

Loading the harvest, c. 1325. Bodleian Library, University of Oxford, Ms. Selden
Supra 38, f.21

Milking sheep, fourteenth century.
Luttrell Psalter, British Library Additional Ms. 42130, f.163v

Men pruning and weeding, second half of fourteenth century.
Bodleian Library, University of Oxford, Ms. D939, section 2, March and April

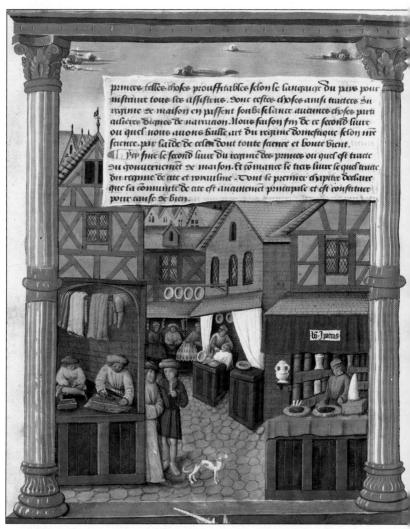

Fifteenth-century shops, on the left a grocer's shop selling sugar loaves and advertizing 'good hippocras'.
Bibliothèque de l'Arsenal, Paris, Ms. 5062, f.149

Woman in kitchen warming her feet.
Corpus Christi College, Oxford, Ms. 285, f.3v

Bellows being used in cooking, fourteenth century.
Bodleian Library, University of Oxford, Ms. Douce 6, f.22

Stalls in street market, Flemish, *c.* 1500.
Bodleian Library, University of Oxford, Ms. Gough Liturg.7, f.11

STOCKS

Stocks market, London in 1598, showing the butchers selling their wares from rails and the fishmongers from 'boordes'.
Hugh Alley's Caveat, Ms. V.a. 318, f.14, Folger Shakespeare Library, Washington

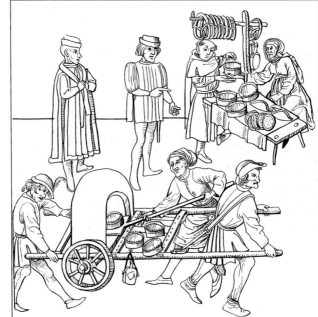

Street sellers, 1417, Constance, Germany. *Concilium Constantiense*, St Petersburg, 1874

Butcher's shop, man preparing sausages, early fourteenth century.
Bodleian Library, University of Oxford, Ms. Douce 5, f.7

Baker's shop, with baker removing loaves with a wood 'pele'. Bodleian Library,
University of Oxford, Ms. Canon Liturg.99, f.16

Dishonest baker drawn through the street on hurdle with the light-weight loaf round his neck. Drawing from the thirteenth-century *Liber de Assisa Panis*, City of London (David Scuffam)

7 li bien se prouuoit 7 estoit si cremus
Q ua senseigue porter su sor tous esleus
7 aymes lenkierka qui niert mie espous
T ant itrencha de hyaumes tant ipcha descus

Cooking operations in the open air, from left to right using the mortar (large and small), pots being heated over different parts of the fire to give different levels of heat, *c.* 1340. Bodleian Library, University of Oxford. Ms. 264 part 1, f. 170v.

Tavern scene showing cellar.
British Library Additional Ms. 27695, f.14

Cooks outside the 'Saltire' inn, c. 1340. Bodleian Library, University of Oxford, Ms. 264, f.83v

Pot suspended over a fire from ratchet mechanism allowing the height above the fire to be altered, man using a kitchen fork.
Pierpont Morgan Library, New York, M638, f.20v

Washing up. Drawing from a wood carving in Kirby Thorpe church, Yorkshire (David Scuffam)

Puzzle jug, polychrome ware, Saintonge, France, late thirteenth century.
Exeter City Museums

Royal banquet, John of Gaunt feasting with the King of Portugal, 1386. Note the bench for the bishops to sit on and the chair of state for Guant, the honoured guest. British Library Ms. Royal 14EIV, f.244v

Trencher of beech, sixteenth century, English, with wooden and pewter spoons.
Board of Trustees of the Victoria and Albert Museum

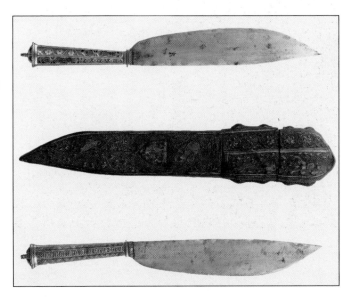

Banquet for a bride, served by the carver under a baldaquin of honour, in the gallery musicians and on the right the cupboard or sideboard, c. 1470. Bibliotheque de L'Arsenal, Paris, Ms 5072 f140

Medieval pottery, showing (left to right) 'face jug' for the table (fourteenth century), dish, table jug, table jug, storage jar, drinking horn (fourteenth century), storage jar. London Museum

Hand-washing before a meal.
Drawing from a thirteenth-century
manuscript (David Scuffam)

Burghley *Nef*, made from a nautilus shell mounted in silver parcel gilt, French, 1482. Board of Trustees of the Victoria and Albert Museum

Standing salt in form of an eagle, English, 1570.
Board of Trustees of the Victoria and Albert Museum

Sixteenth-century banquet, perhaps showing the chaos normally obtaining, rather than the calm prescribed by etiquette. *Banchetti Compositione di Vivande*, 1549. The Hulton Deutsch Collection

Banquet scene, the noblest person at the feast is being served with bread by the panter, who is using his broad knife. In front of the lord are the bread trenchers, arranged according to the rules of etiquette. There is an elaborate salt to his left and he is eating one to a mess, the dish in front of him. The others seem to be eating from round trenchers, at about four to a mess, some of them using spoons. The food is being introduced by wind instruments. The 'cupboard' in the background is covered with plate.
Der Schatzbehalter, Nuremberg, 1491

State banquet with the Duc de Berry as a principal guest. In front of him are his great golden salt (decorated with his swan and bear badges) and his carver with a towel over his left shoulder, as prescribed by the etiquette books. Trés Riches Heures du Duc de Berry, Calendrier, Janvier: le Duc de Berry à table (avec zodiaque) Ms. 65/1284, f.1v, Giraudon

Dancing at a banquet, mid-fifteenth century, the man 'serving' the head of John the Baptist is using a napkin as prescribed by etiquette. Giovanni di Paolo, National Gallery, London

Minstrels of the fourteenth century playing a dulcimer (portable organ), a bagpipe and a fiddle. (David Scuffam)

Musician playing nakers. Luttrell Psalter, fourteenth century, British Library, Additional Ms. 42130, f.176

to have good properties, as indeed it has. It was also thought to be good for fevers, and for the chest and lungs, although some thought it could cause disease. As Drummond and Wilbraham said, since the quality of milk, particularly that supplied in towns, must sometimes have been very low, if not full of infection, a degree of caution was very wise. Butter was also a highly regarded part of the diet, although it was used chiefly in cooking. A great deal of it seems to have been used in a clarified form, as a semi-liquid, made by a process that would have destroyed most, if not all, of the vitamin A it contained, although it might have increased the vitamin D content. Since this process would also have made it rancid, it is difficult to see why it was thought to be a good thing to use.

Other health problems could have been caused by the generally poor hygiene, and by the vessels used for cooking. Lead could leach from pewter vessels (made from an alloy of tin and lead) if acid liquids such as vinegar were kept in them. In the sixteenth century the new tinned copper pots could have poisoned the user once the tin had worn off. The water, too, was probably often hazardous. The streets were often in a filthy state, despite the town authorities' efforts. The rubbish, which often included offal, must have decomposed and washed into the water courses and wells, creating potent sources of infection.[24]

Whatever the balance of the different foods eaten, and their level of purity, the basic diet of medieval people, whether rich or poor, was cereal in the form of bread and ale, and as much meat (or fish) as they could buy or otherwise obtain. This is obviously an oversimplified picture, particularly in the case of the rich since the variety of food available was very wide. The range of food eaten did change over the period dealt with here, though not to a very large extent. In the fourteenth century in London, for example, there were considerably more bakers making brown bread than white (a proportion of 32 to 21), but there was later a change towards more white-bread bakers. Similarly there is evidence from Winchester that in the early fourteenth century there were more fishmongers than butchers, while after 1350 the trend was reversed. It may be that the burghers were eating more meat as they became wealthier, although they were still obliged by the church to eat as much fish as before. There was also a dramatic increase in butchery in London at the end of the fourteenth century. In towns, as in the country, the consumption of bacon declined and more beef and mutton were eaten. This increase in meat-eating is also illustrated by the fact that, in the early fifteenth century, builders were receiving nearly 40 per cent of their diet in the form of non-cereal food as part of their pay. There is little doubt that peasants at least were better paid and fed by the fifteenth century. By the sixteenth century, in 1548, servants of Sir William Petre were receiving a few pounds of beef every week, roughly one thirtieth of an ox.[25]

This apparent change in diet, for some of the population at least, does not affect the conclusions that may be drawn about the nutrition of the population. The chief difficulty is finding out what people ate normally, rather than just at banquets, which are relatively well documented but for which the number of people present and the volume of food served is rarely (if ever) known. Some details of the meals that the rich would have expected to eat have already been given, for example from the household regulations of the Earl of Northumberland, and there are other sources, both clerical and lay. Household regulations giving these proposed meals occur at intervals from the fourteenth to the sixteenth centuries and although the diet had undoubtedly begun to change towards the end of the century, the food consumed in the first half in, for example, the royal household of Henry VIII was very similar to that of earlier centuries.

An attempt will be made below to demonstrate the

probable nutrition level of different groups of the population and what food made up their diet. There are quite a number of documents that indicate, to a greater or lesser extent, what various households ate at each meal. Beginning in the sixteenth century, the diet dictated by Henry VIII for himself and for his household in 1527 was very lavish, at least for the upper levels, and much the same as that ordained for the household of Henry Percy in 1512.[26] There is no question that most, if not all, of the household had enough to eat. They would certainly have consumed sufficient to maintain an active life, while for the King and Queen, and others of high rank, it would have been easy for them to have too much (although it has been pointed out that pictures of fat people are rare for medieval and early modern Europe). The King had no less than twenty-three dishes in the two courses laid down for his dinner on a flesh day, and even more on a fish day. Supper took a similar form. No vegetable dishes are mentioned, although there would have been vegetables and herbs in the stews and pottages. Each meal ended with fruit, sometimes unspecified, sometimes quinces, Pippins, 'dowcetts' (a type of sweet apple) and always oranges. Butter and eggs were also specifically mentioned. Butter was similarly allowed for in the Percy household.[27] Considerable amounts of bread, ale and wine were also allowed. A similar diet, on a less lavish scale (considerably less lavish lower down), applied throughout the household. Fruit was to be supplied to all in the form of apples or 'fruit' (never as oranges except for the royal table), except to the lesser servants such as grooms, porters, maids and 'scowerers'. Eggs and butter were omitted from these diets too. The total quantity of food was probably adequate, but it is difficult to be sure since the amounts (of beef and mutton, for instance) were not specified, nor was the size of the mess (or group) in which they ate. No fruit was specified in the diets of the Northumberland household or for the household of Sir William Petre in 1552, but considerable amounts of butter, cheese and eggs were mentioned.[28] Fruit, including lemons, oranges and strawberries (no less than three pints of these latter at one time), was frequently eaten for supper, and lettuce, as a salad for dinner, was eaten by William Darrell in 1589, but this is rather later than the 'medieval' period. It is interesting that these items were being eaten by this time.[29]

Accounts also exist for the earlier centuries. Those described so far belonged to lay households. Representing the fifteenth century are the diet rolls of St Swithin's Priory, Winchester.[30] These date from the 1490s and are laid out by the day, but each list usually says against most of the dishes at which meal they were eaten. As before, there is no doubt that the volume of food eaten would have provided sufficient protein, carbohydrate and fat. Each day the monks ate about 1½ lb of meat plus two or three other courses with each meal, together with bread and ale. In season they ate quite a few mushrooms, and on most days at least 150 eggs between them (occasionally as many as 400), which was equal to at least five each, given that there were about thirty monks at this time. They also ate a large amount of vegetable broth and occasionally stuffed vegetables (they had the latter on Christmas Day). Much shellfish was eaten also. There is no mention of fruit except 'pomey' (probably an apple dish of some kind), which was used as an entrée, although the monks of Westminster certainly ate fresh fruit when in season. Milk is mentioned infrequently, and then without a cost, as being 'from Berthon'. This consumption of milk from 'the manor' (and not charged for), as opposed to milk bought (which was also mentioned), is also found in the accounts of the Countess of Leicester in 1265. It seems likely that in some cases, if it was no one's responsibilty to account for it, food such as milk or vegetables could be eaten without them appearing on the accounts.[31]

Other fifteenth-century diets (those of the Bryene and

Bridport chantry households) were discussed in Chapter 3. These gave even less detail of the meals eaten. For the fourteenth century, however, there exist two very interesting diets for military personnel which at last give an idea of the quantities eaten. One is for two English garrisons in Scotland in about 1300, the other for Venetian marines in 1310.[32] Presumably these diets were intended to maintain the men in a fit state for fighting, and thus represent at least what the ruling authorities thought was an adequate diet. From the total amounts supplied and the number of men in the garrisons, it is possible to calculate that each man was supplied with about 2 lb of wheat flour, nearly 1 gallon of ale, 1½ lb of fish (herrings and stockfish) or, on meat days, about 1 lb of beef (or pork), and 10 oz of pottage made from peas, beans and oatmeal. They also had cheese, butter, onions, garlic (but apparently no other vegetables) and various spices. In one case about ⅓ gallon of wine was allowed per day. From these figures it may be shown that each man was given food that gave about 5,000 calories a day. This was quite high (the level recommended for a moderately active adult man is 3,000+ calories), but not excessive for active men, as these presumably were. The meat allowance may be compared with just under ½ lb of meat allowed to the clerics in the household of the Archbishop of Arles in 1429.

The other military diet, for Venetian marines, was quite similar when considering the differences in country. These soldiers were given (at least in theory) 1½ lb of biscuit, nearly 1½ oz of cheese, nearly 2 oz of salt pork and 3½ oz of beans. The latter two were taken in the form of a soup. To these were added nearly a pint of wine. This would have provided nearly 4,000 calories a day. Though rather less than for the English soldiers, this was still more than adequate.[33] There is no indication that any further vegetables were allowed, nor that fish was substituted for pork on fast days. Other, later (sixteenth-century) military rations were like these two examples.[34] These military diets are probably similar to those enjoyed by moderately wealthy and rich peasants. The maintenance agreements for elderly peasants (see Chapter 2) give some idea as to the diet regarded as common by these groups, although the range of food supplied in these agreements was very wide.[35] Most only gave the quantity of grain (wheat frequently, but sometimes other grains, barley, oats, rye and various mixtures of them). Pulses were occasionally specified also. In the majority of agreements, the grain would have been enough to provide an adequate amount of food and drink (with ale being made from the barley, and bread from the other grains). In some cases the amounts would have been inadequate to support even a sedentary life. As already discussed, working peasants at least frequently did supplement their diet with meat (in the form of bacon), vegetables, milk, cheese and eggs. This was, in many ways, a much better diet than that of the very wealthy, who probably ate few dairy products as such, at least until the sixteenth century.

The two military diets give a good idea of the basic diet of all classes, as well as the actual diets of two particular groups. It is clear that they offered the necessary fuel. Whether they contained sufficient nutriment, however, is another matter. Food consists of fat, carbohydrate, protein, and small amounts of vitamins and minerals. The diets of most classes would usually have contained satisfactory proportions of fat, protein and carbohydrate. The gentry tended to eat too much meat and would thus have had a very high protein intake, but there is no firm evidence that this excess would necessarily have been bad. Conversely a low protein intake is bad, in that it can cause many problems, including poor growth. Fat and carbohydrate were unlikely to have been consumed to excess except in the households of the higher nobility. The danger of this was obesity (which causes its own problems). For a few there may have been some justification, since a high calorie intake was more necessary for those living in a cold and draughty manor or castle. The mineral intake was probably reasonably sufficient, although it has been suggested for an ecclesiastical household in France that the diet would have been low in calcium due to a lack of dairy products in the diet. Since they would probably have eaten as much fish (some of which, herring for example, contain a considerable amount of calcium) as laymen, if not more, this deficiency seems unlikely. There is a small amount of evidence for mineral imbalance in the medieval diet (see below), but this occurs even in modern society. Fibre, which is also necessary in a healthy diet, was likely to have been more than adequately represented in the diet of ordinary peasants and townsfolk, since their bread would have had a high proportion of bran. Even the bread of the gentry and nobility would have contained more fibre than modern bread. In addition, the great deal of dried fruit eaten contained much fibre. It is interesting to note that the estimated daily diet given by Drummond and Wilbraham for the fifteenth-century peasant and 'meat-eating classes' shows sufficient carbohydrate, protein and minerals for both classes, with far too much protein for the latter. These estimates can be criticized in that it is unlikely that all peasants drank a pint of milk and a pint of whey each day, and no ale is mentioned. However, the quantities of the different foods suggested for both classes are corroborated by various sources: that of the peasant by the diet of the Venetian marines, for example; and that of the 'meat-eating class' by the Northumberland household book. Another interesting point is that, apart from low levels of vitamin C, the estimated amount of vitamins is considered sufficient.[36]

The main problem with discussing medieval diet is in deciding whether enough vitamins were consumed. Since it is not feasible to calculate with any degree of accuracy the amount of food eaten, it is equally impossible to calculate the amount of any particular vitamin. However, knowing the type of food eaten, it is possible to form some idea of whether the amounts taken were likely to have been adequate. There are some thirteen vitamins, all of which are necessary in very small amounts (usually not more than a milligram per day, about the weight of one grain of sugar). Because they are needed in small quantities it is not difficult to obtain the required amount, provided that a balanced diet is eaten. To some extent the medieval diet of the gentry and wealthier classes was balanced, since such a wide range of foods was eaten. Thus, of the B vitamins, riboflavin (vitamin B^2), niacin (nicotinic acid), vitamin B^6 and vitamin B^{12}, are all found in kidney and liver which were frequently eaten in the form of 'numbles' (entrails). They all also occur in eggs, of which very large numbers were eaten. Niacin also occurs in fairly large amounts in ale and beer. The poorer members of society, who might not have had any of these items very often (although niacin does occur in bran and thus in wholemeal bread), might have suffered from niacin deficiency and thus from skin diseases, which do seem to have been prevalent in the Middle Ages (although skin problems can also be caused by a lack of vitamin A). Most of these vitamins also occur in fish, of which large amounts were eaten. The other B vitamin, thiamine (vitamin B^1), also occurs in most fish (and in many other animal and vegetable sources), but not to any large extent in herring, that most frequently eaten.[37]

Other vitamins such as folic acid, biotin, vitamin E and vitamin K also occur in all or some of the foods already mentioned and will thus have been in most diets to some extent. The vitamin pantothenic acid also occurs in most foodstuffs. Large amounts of vitamin A occur in some fatty fish, such as herring and eels, eggs, liver, kidney and milk. The amount of vitamin A from milk and eggs would have been less in the winter when the animals concerned would have been eating less fresh food and so producing less of the vitamin. It is possible that peasants might have had insufficient vitamin A in the winter, since they would probably have eaten fewer herrings than the gentry.[38] The same can be said of vitamin D. This latter is normally formed by the action of sunlight on the skin, but not necessarily in northern countries like England. There is some evidence of vitamin D deficiency in England from burial sites. Few signs of rickets, the chief effect of vitamin D deficiency, have been found for this period (though it was common in later centuries), although pitting of the skull, another possible effect, has been found. However, this has been attributed to iron deficiency anaemia, which was apparently common during the Middle Ages.[39]

There has been much speculation about whether a deficiency of Vitamin C was particularly prevalent due to a lack of fresh green vegetables and fruit in the diet. Thus it has been suggested that Henry VIII may have suffered from scurvy (the major effect of vitamin C deficiency) in his last few years of life, since his symptoms correspond with this disease. This may be true without it being the case that the deficiency was general. As noted above, the diet of the household of Henry VIII included fresh fruit in the form of apples, oranges and quinces. These all contain vitamin C and, in the case of oranges, in large enough amounts for one orange to supply the daily requirement of one adult. It seems very likely that other households ate fresh fruit too, as described above. It was common to serve fruit as the last course of a banquet. The Goodman of Paris said that oranges were bought for a wedding held in the 1390s. Oranges were imported into England from the late fourteenth century and probably earlier, and must have been bought by those outside the royal household. Royal households had probably always bought fruit. In 1468 the household regulations of the Duke of Clarence ordered that Valencia oranges be bought, as well as pulped quinces. As early as 1285 the 'royal fruiterer' was paid £21 14s. 1½d. for an assortment of fruit that included apples, pears, pomegranates, dried fruit and, in season, cherries. Similar purchases occurred in later years (including plums and again cherries), together with milk and cheese. Some of the dishes in the recipe books also contained raw fruit, for example some versions of the dish known as 'murreye'. The lack of other references to fruit could be because these books were concerned with preparing foostuffs for cooking and would therefore have omitted any reference to fruit that required no preparation.[40]

There was undoubtedly some prejudice against eating raw fruit, and a suggestion that cooking reduced any danger that fruit posed. This was based on the teaching of Galen (of which the doctrine of the humours formed a part), passed on by the *Regimen Sanitatis*, a handbook on health and its preservation. How much the general diet was affected by these doctrines is difficult to say. In 1390 the *Forme of Curye* was compiled with the advice and assent of 'Maisters of phisik and of philosophie', and other cookery books contain similar statements. The doctor of Edward IV was also supposed to be present at all the King's meals to inform him which diet conformed most closely to the recognized rules. It seems most likely, however, that this theoretical advice was ignored as often as similar advice is today.[41] The *Regimen Sanitatis* taught Galen's view that fruit could cause fevers. However, the similar *Tacuinum Sanitatis*, an Arabic health handbook, recommended the eating of fruit in moderation as being useful in various ways depending on the fruit, as did the *Mensa Philosophica* of Michael Scott (written in the thirteenth century). It seems likely that most people ate fruit when it was available as a useful addition to their diet, without paying too much attention to the health handbooks. Scott's work certainly gives the impression that he knew that people would eat fruit despite any dangers. Thus for cherries, which he thought were 'in every way pernicious', he recommended that if they were consumed despite his warnings, they should be eaten on a full stomach which would minimize the problems. Curiously enough it appears that fresh (sour) fruit was recommended as a preventative of the Black Death, together with a diet that, if the sufferer was of a choleric or sanguine disposition, could contain pomegranates, oranges and quinces, as well as fresh vegetables. Other sources suggested a little sour fruit, such as cherries, pomegranates, pears or apples. This advice would have no effect on preventing infection by the plague, but it would undoubtedly have improved the general health.[42]

Fresh fruit would not generally have been available throughout the year, so vitamin C would have to have been obtained from other sources. Considerable numbers of apples were used in cooking, but much, if not all, of the vitamin C would probably have been destroyed through the common practice of over-cooking. Green vegetables also provide vitamin C, but these were not eaten in large amounts. It seems likely that they were eaten in rather larger quantities than has been stated previously though. As mentioned above, recipes for vegetable dishes and salads exist, so there must therefore have been a certain demand for these foodstuffs. Certainly, large amounts of leeks, garlic, cabbage and onions were used in soup. All of these contain vitamin C in relatively large amounts, and at least some would probably have remained even after the typically long cooking period. The other possible source was the large amount of herbs used in the uncooked sauces poured over dishes. These contained, in some cases, such mixtures as parsley, mint, garlic and thyme, all of which contain vitamin C.[43] From all of these possibilities it would appear that the better-off would have obtained enough vitamin C from their diet at least to avoid a serious deficiency. The poorer person would probably have eaten more of the fruit and vegetables that were easy to grow, such as cabbage, turnips, onions and leeks, all containing much vitamin C. From the waxes found in cooking pots it is clear that early medieval peasants ate cabbage, and there is evidence from analysis that the diet of the peasant in the early Middle Ages was low in protein, that is predominantly vegetable matter. This changed to a diet containing more meat as time went by. The remains of cesspits show that strawberries, cherries, apples, gooseberries, bramble fruits, bilberries, sloes (stones from which frequently occur in excavations), damsons and hazelnuts were certainly eaten, presumably regularly. One particular barrel latrine even has grape pips, which may represent fresh grapes or raisins. The fruit would have come from gardens. The richer townsfolk and others had gardens in which they grew fruit and a large range of vegetables (see p. 41). These must have been grown specifically to be eaten – medieval man was a practical person. It has been suggested that since these foods were not usually mentioned in the household accounts (and, given the care with which the accounts were drawn up, their inclusion would have been expected), they were not eaten in significant quantities. This is probably true in many cases, although at least one sixteenth-century steward did not account for fresh fruit, vegetables and herbs that were certainly eaten, and if one steward failed to record these items, there may have been many others. There were some, probably very few, who only ate vegetables. Two such people, in 1297, lived in 'God's House', the almshouse in Southampton in 1297. One of them, Sister Joan, did not eat flesh throughout the year and the other, Sister Elena, 'ate nothing that had suffered death'.[44]

It seems probable, therefore, that most of the population of medieval England would have received enough vitamins in their diet to remain reasonably healthy throughout the year.

It is possible that some would have been in a prescorbutic condition towards the end of the winter, when no fresh fruit and few fresh vegetables would have been available for some time. The amount of food eaten would probably have been enough for many, although those at the bottom of the social pyramid would sometimes have gone hungry. What the quality of the food was like remains a matter for speculation. It has also been suggested that many would have been at risk of alcoholism, but that is another matter.[45]

SIX

TABLE MANNERS

Good table manners were important in the Middle Ages. This was particularly true for the higher ranks of society who had more time to consider such niceties, but it also applied to some extent to the poorer members of the community. There is evidence that some peasant households used, for example, tablecloths, napkins and towels, arising from the fact that they were noted as having been stolen. Knives for eating with were common since they were routinely carried as an everyday part of their dress, at least by the men, and spoons were also used in the peasant household. The people ate from wooden bowls and platters, probably in many cases made by the users. Large amounts of earthenware were used for cooking and eating from, probably because it was generally cheap, although some of it seems to have been of finer quality. Metal pots, too, were used, these latter frequently made of brass and sometimes of considerable value compared with the rest of a peasant's chattels, for example 2s. 6d. (12p) for a pot, probably of 1 or 2 gallons capacity, compared with a farm cart worth 7d. (3p). Cooking was done over a fire, sometimes on a metal sheet (to prevent the fire from spreading) or outside the house. It was usually carried out in a metal cauldron, sometimes using a trivet or a gridiron. From 1380 an inventory of the goods of a villager listed pans, a cresset, a tripod, a skillet, colanders and five silver spoons as kitchen utensils. These were valued at £2. Peasants also washed their hands after eating (and, one supposes, sometimes before eating as well), since one ten-year-old boy drowned himself in a market place trough in which he was washing his hands and his bowl after eating.[1] Peasants also washed themselves and their clothing. Drunkenness was occasionally a problem in the village, but, while this shows a lack of manners, it adds little to our knowledge of how peasants behaved. It does show that some of them, at least, had sufficient money to spare to get drunk.

The behaviour of the nobility is much better documented and demonstrates the great importance attached to good table manners, or perhaps conventional table manners. There is a great deal of evidence for the behaviour expected, the best known of which are books of courtesy. These were partly intended for the education of servants, so the books said (although it is difficult to believe that most of them would either have had the opportunity or the ability to read them), and partly for the young squires or 'yonge babees'. The master of the henchmen (in charge of the squires or henchmen) taught these youths 'how manerly they ete and drinke', educating them to act as pages to serve at table and carve, and do body service to their lord. The books also seem to have been partly for those adults not so sure of the behaviour expected of them. Most, if not all, seem to date from the fifteenth to sixteenth centuries.[2] It is difficult to know how wide a circle these books reached, or indeed how well qualified some of their authors were to write them, although some of them undoubtedly were (see below). The books dealt with many aspects of behaviour, including the duties of parents and masters, the manner of serving a knight or gentleman, ordering one's master's bedroom and good manners. The assumption here, in the discussion of table manners, is that those described were current for much of the period from *c.* 1250 to *c.* 1550. This is not entirely true, but it is probably true that the behaviour expected on formal occasions was not so very different throughout the period, apart from an increasing elaboration. Any bias in the description will be towards the fifteenth century from which the best sources come.

Before considering manners, however, what were the mealtimes and how often did people eat in a day? The very poor doubtless ate when they could, but the slightly better-off peasants seem generally to have eaten three times a day. These meals consisted of breakfast at a very early hour to allow for dinner at about 9.00 a.m., or not later than 10.00 a.m., and supper probably before it got dark, perhaps at 3.00 p.m. in the winter. The times and number of meals were originally derived from the hours of devotions of the Church. Monks ate the main meal of their day after the celebration of nones, which was nine hours after daybreak. This was in practice at some time between midday and 3.00 p.m. The evening meal had to be a reasonable time after this, at or after vespers (around sunset). Three meals a day were accepted as reasonable by most later sixteenth-century writers, such as Andrew Borde, although he thought that this was only good for the labouring man: anyone else should be content with two. It has been suggested that breakfast was only eaten by children and workmen, but certainly by the fifteenth century it was quite commonly taken by everyone. Breakfast was regularly allowed for in the accounts of Dame Alice de Bryene at the beginning of the fifteenth century, although the 1478 household ordinance of Edward IV specifies that only residents down to the rank of squires should have breakfast, except by special order. Edward, Prince of Wales, son of Edward IV, breakfasted after morning mass. The time was only specified as 'a convenyent hower', although to break one's fast after devotions was the generally recommended procedure. Earlier references to breakfast sometimes meant dinner, literally, in these cases, the first meal of the day.[3] Sir William Harrison thought that in previous times (not specified) there had been four meals eaten a day, that is breakfast, dinner, 'nuntions' (or 'nuncheons', taken at about noon) and late supper. Nuncheons was usually something eaten by workmen who were given payment for it. The Earl of Northumberland dined at noon in 1512, but he also had a meal in the afternoon known as 'drynkyngs', as did other noble lords. Sometimes a late meal, the 'reresoper', was eaten in the evening. This indulgence, which often included much wine, was frowned on by moralists. Edward, Prince of Wales (son of Edward IV), probably dined at 11.00 a.m. (the servants dined at 10.00 a.m.) and supped at 5.00 p.m., (the servants at 4.00 p.m.). On fast days the servants dined at 11.00 a.m. These times were the same as those observed by the Prince's grandmother, Cecily, Duchess of York. The staggering of meals in large households, with the servants eating earlier than the lord (and some of them later in very large households), was common. In Edward IV's court, 12 of his 24 squires dined before he did and 12 after, and the same at supper, 'soo that atte lest xij be ever redy to serve the king and the quene when it shall plese them to be served'.[4]

Having established when people ate, we can consider the arrangements for a formal meal and the table manners expected of those taking part. The various descriptions that exist are not clear and frequently conflict, so the following description is based on several versions. The best place to start is with the laying of the table. This was performed by several officials who first of all arrayed the 'cupboard' by covering it with a cloth. The cupboard (occasionally known as the dresser, although this was more of a piece of kitchen equipment) was a fairly simple piece of furniture. It usually consisted of a number of shelves (frequently three) in a frame about 6 feet high and 4 feet wide. A cupboard (in the modern sense) was built below the top shelf. Regulations exist that specify that the higher the rank in society, the more shelves were allowed, with a duke allowed five shelves and a knight only one. This custom was probably honoured more in the breach than in the observance, although Cardinal Wolsey apparently had one with six shelves, thus ranking above a duke, and Henry VIII had one with eight shelves. The cupboard was then decked with as much gold and silver plate as the household could muster to impress guests, so that it would be 'greatly coveted of many that sawe it'.

A cloth was laid over the left arm of the people setting the table and a towel about their neck, 'for that is curtesy'.[5] After this the table was wiped and covered with a 'feyre and clene' cloth. In the best households the cloth used for the lord was made from the finest linen, which was much admired. The lesser members of the household had lower grade or older linen, or, indeed, none at all. The linen for the cloth and for the napkins was often bought in bulk and the cloths made up from it. The regulations for laying the cloth were very elaborate and far from clear. There is evidence that there was sometimes more than one cloth (up to three), possibly because the standard width of a piece of cloth (at 63 inches) was too narrow to cover a table properly and to have it hanging down as was desired. This seems to have been achieved by laying one piece from end to end of the long table and the other laid so as to hang one over each side. The actual laying was done by two staff, one using a rod to smooth out wrinkles, and both to stretch the cloth between them. The regulations for the household of Henry VII envisage the King being seated before the cloth was laid.[6] It has been suggested that a table carpet was laid on the table before the cloth, although this does not seem to be supported by any English source. It is not clear whether or not the cloth was ironed, although it seems unlikely that a crumpled and unironed cloth would have been admired and the care taken to smooth out the wrinkles indicates that the cloth was ironed. In the Middle Ages the tables were most likely to be made from trestles, to make clearing them away afterwards easier. Covering them was thus a necessity. By the fifteenth century the high table was sometimes permanent, but by then the lord probably only dined in the hall with the rest of the household on very great occasions, more usually dining in a privy chamber with his close associates. It is not clear how often the lord dined in the hall before the fifteenth century. He was certainly expected to do so in the thirteenth century. Bishop Grosteste (or whoever wrote his 'Rules'), in about 1235, believed that servants should be made to eat in the hall, and that the lord should do so too to show himself in public and to supervise the staff. The type of service expected by the bishop was recognizably similar to that of later 'rules'. Those attending the meal sat on benches, while the lord and his special guests sometimes sat in chairs of estate, and usually with cushions. In the case of Archbishop Neville in the late fifteenth century, his cushions were made of silk.[7]

After the cloth had been laid, a trencher of bread, a napkin and (sometimes) a clean spoon were set out for each person expected to eat. Laying the table could thus be done after the guests were seated if there were a great many of them. Sometimes a cup and loaf were given to each person. John Russell (in the early fifteenth century) noted that the lord had new bread (the upper crust was particularly reserved for the lord) and others had one-day-old bread. The household staff had three-day-old bread and the trenchers were made from that which was four days old. Trenchers of bread were superseded by those of wood or metal in the course of the sixteenth century. Those of the peasants seem to have been of wood, probably from much earlier than this, since in 1314 the custumal of the village of Northcory in the diocese of Wells said that at the Christmas celebration one villein had to bring with him his own trencher. Since bread was supplied as part of the feast, the implication here is that the trencher was wood.[8] It was important that bread was cut squarely and tidily. The loaf was round when made, but a square shape was regarded as much more elegant. The Goodman of Paris wrote that trencher bread should be of brown bread 6 inches wide and 4 inches high, but it is not clear if this was before or after cutting. The carver was in charge of cutting the trenchers for the lord. With his knife he cut off pieces from the bread, as well as the trencher for another member of the staff, to 'assay', that is to test for poison. He touched another piece of bread in the salt, then with his hand 'make a floryshe over it' and passed it on for assay as well. Testing for poison was probably only done for great lords; it is hard to imagine it being thought necessary in other households. After this the carver cut four trenchers and laid them before his lord in a quadrant on top of which he laid three small pieces of bread. He was enjoined to use his broad knife to move the bread and to hold it in his napkin, thus avoiding any touch. These trenchers were cut carefully and presented to the lord on the point of the knife.[9]

The main salt cellar was then laid before, or on the right hand of, the lord with the trenchers on the left of this. In noble households this salt was the great salt cellar, frequently of silver and of splendid design. These cellars were often of great value and were sometimes mentioned in wills. Such was the silver salt cellar in the shape of a dog from the will of Edmund Earl of March, in 1380, or the gold one mentioned in the will of John of Gaunt, in 1397, embellished with a garter. Those in royal collections were particularly fine, for example that owned by Edward II, in 1324, in the form of a silver ship (*nef*) on four wheels with a castle at each end in gold. The *nef* was particularly popular on the Continent, which may be where the 'grand nief' found by Henry IV in the royal treasury came from. This was valued at £68 and was of silver gilt on lion's feet with (among much else) eight men at arms holding banners and pennons of the arms of France in an embattled turret, also of silver gilt.[10] The salt used in the cellar was more or less pure, depending on the source and its aftertreatment. In the Middle Ages most salt came from the evaporation of brine (from natural salty springs) or sea water. None of it was mined. Much of it came from the west coast of France (most of it from the Bay of Bourgneuf, known as 'Bay' salt), where it was prepared by allowing the sun to evaporate shallow pools of sea water. This process gave very impure salt, so it was frequently purified by merchants before sale, or by fastidious households before use, by redissolving, filtering and evaporating it again. Purer salt for table or dairy use was more often bought as such, while 'Bay' salt was often only used for curing. Salt was given to the lord by the carver who spread some on a trencher.[11]

On the left of his place was set the lord's knife with some white bread by its side. The bread of the lord was wrapped in a napkin with an open end towards him. The knife and napkin were first kissed and wiped 'for assay'. One source gives as much as eight loaves, or buns, for the lord's bread. Presumably they were not full-size loaves. This bread was the best manchet, while guests of lower status received lower quality bread.[12] Knives were sometimes only supplied to the lord and possibly to his honoured guests; others were expected to bring their own. The spoon (for use with soups and semi-liquid dishes) was wrapped in a napkin and then all was covered with another napkin. Guests frequently brought their own spoon, usually of horn but sometimes of silver. Forks were rarely used in England before the sixteenth century, except for sweetmeats and perhaps for carving the meat.[13]

The final ceremony before the meal could commence was washing the hands. A towel ('surnape') was laid on the tablecloth, with elaborate ceremony in great households, to protect it. Then the lord and his guests were presented with the water. That for the lord was first of all tasted by the cupbearer (if there was one) and the towel kissed. The cup used for this purpose was sometimes made from agate, or lined with it, since it was believed to change colour when poison was added. Unicorn horn (narwhal tooth), which was also believed to change colour in the presence of poison, was sometimes used too. This ceremonial hand-washing was probably little more than nominal, while that after the meal might have been different, although much emphasis was laid on having clean hands in the Curtesy Books. Hot and cold water were provided, sometimes scented. It was either poured over the hands from above (which could be a hazardous proceeding), or the hands were put into the water. It is arguable whether or not hand-washing was for reasons of hygiene as well as for good manners, but there seems little doubt that concepts of hygiene played some part in the ceremony. Whatever the reason for the hand-washing, afterwards the surnape was removed, the bread and table implements uncovered and the bread cut for the lord.[14]

At some point in the proceedings, perhaps just before the food appeared, grace was said. It is not mentioned in the ceremony at Archbishop Neville's feast of 1466, but in the fifteenth-century *Boke of Curtasye* and the later *For to Serve a Lord* it is placed just after the hand-washing. The first dish could then be brought in by the carver, or in some households he followed the main dish into the hall. The food was first tasted and then handed out, or carved for the lord and for his guests. The carving had to be done in a prescribed manner, the instructions specifying that hands and knives should be clean and the knife sharp and held in the correct manner: 'holde alwey thy knyfe sure, thy self not to tene, and passe not ij fyngurs and a thombe on thy knyfe so kene; In mid wey of thyne hande set the ende of the haft sure unlasynge and mynsynge ij fyngurs with the thombe that may ye endure'. The food was to be held with the left hand and cut with the right. All varieties of meat, fowl, fish and so on had their own prescribed method of carving. There were special terms that were used when describing the carving (for example, 'splatting a pike' and 'undertranch a porpoise'), and rules about how each animal should be presented after carving. The more difficult items, such as crab ('a slut to kerve and a wrawd [ungoodly] wight'), needed to be sent back to the kitchen for reheating before they were served. Slices of bread could be used by the sewer to protect his hands from a dish that was too hot to hold. The carver also added the sauces where necessary.[15]

While the guests were eating it was important for the servants to be ready to take fragments of food from the trenchers. This was done with a trencher knife. The panter, or his colleague the butler, had three knives: one to cut the bread, one to pare the pieces and one to smooth the trenchers. These fragments were put into the 'voyder' (receptacle) which was kept at hand. The voiders had to be emptied regularly before they became full. When the lord's trencher was wet it was removed from the table, and similarly when guests had stopped eating the first and second courses. Courses had to be removed quickly and sauces taken away with them. It was generally expected that the table would be kept as clean and tidy as possible during a meal.[16]

Plenty of food and ale had to be supplied because it was important for the lord to appear open-handed and generous. The cups of ale or wine had to be kept full, and the presentation of ale or wine to the guests, as well as to the lord, was accompanied by much ceremony. Wine was frequently drunk watered down. If this was the case it would have been diluted before it was brought to the table, since wine was usually served to the guests (they were neither expected nor allowed to serve themselves). The quality of the wine and the degree of dilution naturally depended on the generosity of the host. Wine cups were occasionally very elaborately and richly made of precious metals, or sometimes of glass, although they were more frequently made of pewter, earthenware or wood. 'Masers' were shallow stemless drinking vessels made of wood. Not everyone drank from cups, it was not uncommon for diners to drink directly from the jug or pitcher, hence the instruction in the books of courtesy to wipe the vessel after use.

When it was obvious that all had finished eating, or that the lord had finished, the table was cleared. This operation began at the lower end, and involved collecting the spoons, then any broth and baked meat left, and last of all the voiders. After this (in 1554), fruit and cheese were served. A clean trencher and knife were used for this course. In the fifteenth century fruit was sometimes served with the main courses, but usually formed part of the last course. This was either cooked or fresh, and eaten together with hippocras (spiced wine), wafers and spices. Sometimes 'clarry' ('clarre') or other types of spiced wine were served. Wines were frequently sweetened, partly because they were often harsh and acid, but also because sweet (and strong) wines were very popular. A general term for spiced and sweetened wines was 'pymentes' (or 'piments'), and recipes for them all are common. They did not differ a great deal. Technically, hippocras was sweetened with sugar and clarry with honey, but the latter was sometimes sweetened with sugar too. The wine used was either red or white, depending on personal preference, and the amount of sweetener and spices varied greatly, although one manuscript source gives three recipes with increasing amounts of spices: *pro populo*, *pro domino* and *pro rege*. Many of the recipes occur not in manuscripts of food recipes but in medicinal manuscripts, indicating that some of them contain *aqua ardente* (alcohol) distilled from wine. This probably reflects the fact that distillation was carried out by the apothecaries during most of the Middle Ages. Many other sweetened drinks existed, for example 'brakott' ('braggot') which was spiced (sometimes sour), and sweetened ale or mead (fermented honey). It is not clear whether these were served at banquets, although it is likely since they are mentioned in the same manuscripts that refer to hippocras. Wafers were served with these drinks. These were made from batter cooked between heated iron moulds, and were savoury (with cheese), spiced or sweetened (with honey). They were sometimes served with small spiced cakes. By the sixteenth century wafers were often replaced by biscuits.

Following this course, all was removed again, and the wine and ale cups were taken away. The remaining fragments were placed in a 'broad' (larger) voider, the trenchers and napkins removed and the table was made tidy again. The last thing to be removed was the salt.[17]

At about this point, in the ecclesiastical household of Archbishop Neville at least, the chaplain removed the alms dish from the cupboard and took it to the table. A loaf had been placed on it which he put onto a trencher that the carver had placed ready. The chaplain then put both trencher and loaf back onto the dish and gave it to the almoner. The giving of alms was an important duty in the Middle Ages. For example, in 1265, the Countess of Leicester fed 800 paupers on three quarters of bread and a tun of cider. All large households had an almoner. The Archbishop's ceremony, or something similar, would have been repeated in other large households and in a less elaborate form in smaller households. In some an alms dish was placed on the table before the lord and the carver placed a loaf in it at the start of the meal 'to serve god fyrst'. In others a small piece of whatever was being served to the lord was placed on the alms dish. In the household of the Duke of Clarence (brother of

Edward IV), the almoner was given 12d. (5p) a month to give to poor people at his discretion, while every day at dinner and supper he was allowed to take every dish that the Duke had finished with (unless he had given it to one of his guests) and give it to the needy, which could include the Duke's own servants if they fulfilled this criterion. In addition, on four or five days every week the almoner distributed other food to the poor at the gate: one 'cheete' (lower quality) loaf between two people, a gallon of ale between eight and a mess of meat for four. He was instructed to see that the food was carefully kept from 'devouringe of dogges'.[18]

The final ceremony of the meal involved presenting the lord with the means to wash his hands. The procedure was similar to that at the beginning of the meal. A clean towel was put on the tablecloth, and basins and ewers were set on it. The diners usually dipped their fingers into the basin, then water was poured over their hands to rinse them. Their hands were dried on a clean napkin handed to them by a servant or page. At this stage of a meal, where the hands would have been greasy and the washing of them more necessary, the napkins used were often older and less ornate than those used at the beginning of the meal. The napkin was of great importance throughout the Middle Ages, more so than later, because of the habit of eating mostly with a knife and fingers. The strict social order was observed in washing the hands, with the lord of the house first, or the senior guest if of higher status. Finally the basin and ewer were taken away and the cloth was taken from the table with the towel wrapped inside. In the sixteenth century if 'conceits' (apples, nuts or cream) were to be provided, another towel was put on the board on which one or two loaves were placed. Trenchers and spoons had to be kept in readiness in case they were needed. Grace was then said. Comfits, sugar and spices were sometimes then served to the lord and his honoured guests in another room.[19]

People's behaviour while eating was supposed to be as elaborately regulated as the serving of the food. The place where someone was seated depended on his status and good manners, and the acute sense of hierarchy in the Middle Ages dictated that he sat in that place. Once the lord was seated the guests sat down. If a trencher loaf had been laid in a guest's place, it was supposed to be cut into two, lengthwise, the top from the bottom. The top crust was then cut into four parts and the bottom into three. All were then put together again. Nothing was eaten until the lord had begun eating, nor until the course had been fully served, lest the guest was thought a glutton. Nor should anyone pare his nails with his knife, which had to be sharp and clean. The knife was not to be wiped on the tablecloth nor the tablecloth played with. When the food was served, making 'soppis' of bread in soup was sometimes frowned on, but sometimes young people were merely enjoined not to put too much bread in the soup before they had tried it in case they left any, as this would have been a waste. The soup spoon was not to be filled too full in case the soup was spilt. The implication here is that a soup or semi-liquid dish was served in individual dishes, not necessarily as part of the recipient's mess (see below). The dishes used may have been the saucers frequently bought by a household. The guest was not expected to blow on the soup (nor on his drink) in case his breath was foul, and care had to be taken to eat and drink quietly at all times. No one was to speak with his mouth full, and spitting or putting his fingers into his cup was to be avoided. Mid-twelfth-century novices apparently sometimes had even worse manners, such as getting rid of the grease on their plate by tipping it onto the table, or removing half-eaten food from their mouth and replacing it on the plate. Such behaviour was denounced. If strangers dined with someone, the food was to be shared. He must never touch their food with his right hand, only with his left. It was not polite for anyone to keep all the good food to himself, much less to take 'the beste morselle'.[20]

Sharing a dish or food with strangers was common due to the system of supplying a number of dishes to a 'mess', that is to a group of people for them to share. This explains the importance of manners, of not putting fingers into a common dish and so on. Only very important people would have eaten alone. The size and amount of food allowed to a mess varied according to status, as did the table position at which one was placed. The number of people to a mess was laid down by John Russell in about 1430, as was much else. He thought (and this presumably corresponded with the practice followed in the household of Humphrey of Gloucester in Russell's time) that anyone of the rank of bishop, mitred abbot, marquess, earl, baron, the Lord Mayor of London or a chief justice could sit two to a mess; knights, abbots, priors, the Master of the Rolls, the Mayor of Calais and such lesser mortals could sit three or even four to a mess; and other ranks, beginning with that of squire, sat four to a mess. The number of dishes varied similarly. Edward III allowed his 'lordes' five dishes to a mess; other gentlemen had three plus pottage; and grooms and others had two. Edward himself had eight dishes. Edward IV ruled in 1478 that every two men in a mess should share a loaf of bread, every four men a gallon of ale and every three men a dish of meat or fish. When it was thought to be for the king's honour (that is on special occasions) every mess of two or three people had half a pitcher of wine. In practice the system of messes seems to have worked by placing dishes containing portions of the main dishes, of soups (unless these were served separately), portions of the roast, and so on in front of the mess, who then helped themselves. The process of sharing a dish with someone else is nowhere very clearly explained.[21]

For similar reasons to the prohibition of crumbling bread into a shared dish, a guest was supposed not to dip his meat into the salt but take it with his fingers or on his knife. The salt should in any case have been put on his trencher, avoiding the need to go to the salt cellar. After finishing soup, the spoon should not be left in the dish but care taken to wipe it clean and lay it down by the side of the trencher. It was important to see that it was not stolen from there. When eating the meat courses, the food was to be cut into small pieces and not torn apart, for that 'swarves from curtesy'. The trencher was not to be filled too full with food, nor the guest's mouth, and he should avoid blowing out crumbs. He was expected not to put food back onto the serving platter. When a sauce was served with the dish, a dab was put onto the trencher and the food dipped into it. Food was not on any account to be dipped into the sauce dish. It was alright, however, for a guest to eat with his fingers, provided that he did not waste food. Bones and other fragments of food that were not wanted were not to be thrown on the ground but carefully put into the voider, along with the napkin. If a dish was taken away before he had finished, no notice should be taken and the guest should certainly not call for it again. When the table was cleared he should hear grace and wash his hands (spitting in the basin was frowned on). On leaving the table (in 1556) each guest was to bow to the lord and withdraw, saying to his companions, 'Much good do it ye'.[22]

As well as indicating the way in which food was to be eaten, the books of courtesy described the expected way of behaving at table. This was apparently sometimes inelegant, to say the least. A guest was not to belch too close to a man's face nor to spit over the table. If necessary, he had to spit on the ground. He was not supposed to pick his teeth with his knife; a toothpick was to be used instead. Using the napkin to blow his nose was frowned upon. A handkerchief was to be used to do this, although it was apparently not unknown for people to use their fingers. In this case they had to wipe their hands on their clothing, not, presumably, on the tablecloth. Guests were not to take the food of other people, nor were they to offer anyone food that they had taken a bite out of. A dish was not to be cleaned out by licking it. Sitting at the table was expected to be decorous, with no one stretching or leaning back on the table, or carving at the table with his knife. A guest was to be quiet and polite, and belching and generally behaving in an obtrusive manner was to be avoided. Staring about, or wagging and scratching his head, particularly as if 'claw[ing] a fleigh', was not good manners, and neither was putting his finger in his mouth. Putting his finger into his nose, as if picking it, was particularly frowned on. Talk and laughter were to be quiet lest anyone should think he was drunk. On the other hand, whispering was bad in case anyone should suspect him of slandering them.[23]

In the higher ranks of society, meals were complicated and labour-intensive operations. The labour was provided by the household. This comprised the large number of servants, household officers and other followers. It naturally varied greatly in size and elaboration depending on the status of the employer, and there is some evidence that, in general, the household increased in size sharply in the early fifteenth century. When the officers of Edward IV drew up a document to show how his household should be organized, they included in it their idea on the costs and size of the smaller households of those of lower status. These ranged from the squire with seven servants, comprising one clerk at £2 a year, two yeomen (or grooms) at the same cost, two lesser servants at £1 a year each, and two boys at 10s. (50p). This would perhaps have been somewhere between the size of the household of the Bridport Chantry priests and that of Alice de Bryene (see Chapter 4). It may be compared with the household of Hamon le Strange (in 1347–8) which included a chaplain, butler, cook, groom, two boys and a lad. These staff looked after Hamon, his wife, Sir John and Lady Camoys (le Strange's mother- and father-in-law), two ladies in waiting and two maids. The Le Strange household was thus between that of the squire and the knight in size. A knight was expected to have 23 in his employment. These included a steward, a young gentleman to look after the table of his lord, and officials to look after specialized aspects of the household activities such as the cooking, the stable, and the falcons and dogs. The total wages were over £10 a year. The household of a baron was expected to number nearly 70, that of an earl around 200 and that of a duke about 250. These figures compare well with some actual households, such as that of the Duke of Clarence in 1468 who had 299. However, John Howard, Duke of Norfolk, appears to have had less than 100 in his household in 1483, some baronial households contained less than 20, and those of some knights up to about 30. The number depended on circumstances, the wealth of the person concerned and on whether the master was at home or travelling.[24] The household taken with the lord when he was travelling between estates (the 'riding household') was much smaller than that usually ministering to his wants in the inner household (the *Hospicium Intrinsecum*). In 1512, for example, that of the Earl of Northumberland numbered 36 instead of the usual 166. In 1420–1 the Earl of Warwick had 55 in his inner household, which also served as that of his countess since he was so infrequently at home. The accounts of the Earl of Warwick's household are interesting in that they demonstrate that, when a household was travelling, stocks of food and wine were moved also. On one occasion in the Berkeley household, a barge was hired to transport the countess's wine and other effects at a cost of £1 15s. (£1.75). Since the wine casks had to be repaired after they had arrived, it might be thought that it would have been more cost- effective to buy the wine on arrival.[25]

The household as a unit became more complicated as it increased in size. As indicated above, a knight's household was of sufficient size for the staff to be given specific tasks. In a very small household, such as that of a squire, the staff would have had to be prepared to turn their hands to virtually any task within their scope. The crucial point would have been that it was within the range of tasks expected from someone of their social standing. The clerk in the esquire's household would not have been expected to work in the kitchen, nor would the lesser servants, who probably worked in the stables as well as the kitchen, have expected to wait at table. The social level at which tasks were carried out moved as the level of the household itself moved up. To take an extreme example, at the coronation banquet of Richard III, the household officers nominally acted as servants. Thus the Earl of Surrey (son of the Duke of Norfolk), Lord Steward and Viscount Lovel, Chamberlain of the household, played a part in serving the banquet.[26] However, the main object of the household remained the same, whatever its size: to supervise the estates of the lord and to maintain his social position. In the context of this book, the household was crucial in providing him with daily services, including those of food and drink. Obviously the number of staff concerned with food varied, but as the size of both household and staff increased, more and more became involved in this area.[27]

The best picture of the offices in a household concerned with food is gained from the royal household. This was naturally the largest example, since, as well as looking after the King and his family, it also contained the personnel of the government. The household consisted of between 400 and 700 people, and exhibited an extreme degree of elaboration and subdivision. There was, for example, even a 'talowe man', who was responsible for the grease collected from animals killed for the kitchen so that the tallow could be made into candles. Smaller, less-exalted households were divided less strictly, so that people would have had several different roles. A description of the royal offices gives an idea of the duties that had to be carried out, however. The royal household was divided into 'offices' according to the work to be done. The pantry distributed the bread and, in theory, made and/or bought it. Later, at least, it was responsible for the napkins, towels and linen for the table, as well as some of the plates, the salts and other utensils. It also encompassed the waferer and the laundresses. The butlery (buttery) supplied and brewed (or bought) the ale and delivered the wine to the table. The cellar stored the wine. The kitchen, with its subordinate departments, bought, prepared and delivered the food. The larder was responsible for the meat and fish, which was provided by the 'acatry', where the tallow man worked. The 'poultry' provided the poultry, the scullery the pots, pans and other cooking vessels, together with wood and coal necessary, the 'saucery' made the sauces for the foods, and worked closely with the 'pastry', and the 'spicery' received the spices from the 'great wardrobe' and distributed them as necessary. Some of these departments themselves had sub-departments, such as the scaldinghouse which was under the control of the office of poultry. It is disputed how far these offices were in fact separate departments, and the divisions between them varied over the years.[28]

The arrangements in the kitchen varied in elaboration, depending on the size of the household. Cooking was carried out over charcoal, usually produced on the estate. 'Sea coal' was not generally used in England until the middle of the sixteenth century. Vast amounts of fuel were used when cooking for a feast. For example, in 1403 a thousand cartloads of dry wood and a 'large barnful of coal' was suggested for a two-day occasion in Savoy. For the same event a most interesting list of equipment needed in the kitchen was drawn up. This appears to be unique and was as follows:

There should be a provision of good cauldrons to boil large cuts of meat, and a great number of moderate sized ones for making pottages and for other cooking operations, and great suspended pans for cooking fish and other things and a great number of large and ordinary sized boilers for pottages and other things and a dozen good big mortars. . . . And you will need some twenty large frying pans, a dozen great kettles, fifty pots, sixty two-handled pots, a hundred hampers, a dozen grills, six large graters, a hundred wooden spoons, twenty five holed spoons, both large and small, six pot-hooks, twenty oven shovels, twenty roasters, both those with turntable spits and those with spits mounted on andirons. You should not put your trust in wooden skewers or spits, because you could spoil all your meat, or even lose it; rather you should have six score iron spits which are strong and thirteen feet long; and you need three dozen other spits which are just as long but not as thick, in order to roast poultry, piglets and water birds. . . . And besides this, four dozen slender skewers for doing glazing and for fastening things.

The pot hooks in this list were for suspending pots over the fire at different heights, depending on the degree of heat required. Some of the pots were on tripod legs of their own to stand over the fire. Trivets and gridirons to support pots appeared on some inventories. The oven shovels were to put dishes in and take them out of the ovens. They may also have been used as baking shovels held over the fire. Food was sometimes baked on the hearth in front of the fire. Long-handled frying pans were used in a similar way to the baking shovels. The mortars were among the most useful equipment in the kitchen, since much of the food was pounded to a pulp before it was cooked. It is odd that there is no mention of the useful jack, for automatically turning a spit, which was in use at this time.

With this list were instructions for a large amount of fine white cloth to cover the tables and food, and some for straining jellies and hippocras. Also required to prepare the food were two large two-handled knives to cut up the oxen, 'a dozen dressing knives for dressing and two dozen knives for cutting up ingredients for pottages and for stuffings and to prepare poultry and fish'. Also needed were six rasps to clean work tables and chopping blocks, baskets to carry raw and cooked meat to and from the large double work tables (the tables had to have space between to allow the kitchen squires to walk to and fro), and up to 4,000 dishes (of gold, silver, pewter and wood) so that, when the first serving had been made, there would be enough left over to use for the second. Before the third course the dirty dishes from the first would have been cleaned, probably by scouring them with sand, although this is not mentioned as needed.[29]

SEVEN

FEASTS

The culmination of medieval meal preparation and eating were the great feasts given by monarchs, princes and high-ranking prelates on suitable occasions. Many occasions were regarded as suitable: religious festivals, such as Christmas or the end of Lent; or secular ones, such as the end of harvest or sheep shearing. The main purpose of a feast was a celebration, and a formal feast was part of all ceremonies, such as coronations and receptions. These feasts demonstrated the wealth and taste of the host and reaffirmed his place in the social hierarchy. The host showed his importance and his power, and the guests showed by their presence that they played a part in the hierarchy. This was emphasized by the elaborate ceremonies that formed an integral part of the feast. The social hierarchy was also reinforced by the order in which the participants sat. In the extreme, a coronation banquet for example, eating was a spectacle, the spectators at a feast playing as important a part (if gaining less satisfaction) as those eating and drinking. Major feasts were certainly not common – cost and the logistics of bringing together the vast resources needed, saw to that – and, of course, not all feasts were elaborate.

Occasions could easily be manufactured for a feast, such as in Calais in 1478 when the married men of the wool Staple challenged the bachelors to an archery match over a distance of 260 yards. The losers had to pay for a meal costing 12d. (6p) per head each.[1]

Owing to the importance of the larger feasts and the contemporary interest taken in them, a great many records exist. Large feasts needed a great deal of forward planning and there is a certain amount of information on this. It is not known how soon the menu was decided. This may have occurred late in the day, but the approximate quantities of the usual major ingredients, such as bread, wine and meat, would have been known from previous occasions, and arranging for these undoubtedly started some time beforehand. The planning for one major feast in the thirteenth century has been analysed, and the results are very interesting. The occasion was the marriage of Margaret, daughter of Henry III, to Alexander III of Scots at York on 26 December 1251. Planning began at least by the summer, and by the end of July, beasts were being bought in York and other fairs, with orders for them to be pastured until needed. They were not slaughtered until just before the wedding. At about the same time orders for the catching, slaughtering and salting of 300 red and fallow deer were issued. In November nearly 1,000 more roe, fallow and red deer were ordered. In the meantime, in October, the sheriffs of the northern counties were ordered to supply the other flesh meat needed in the shape of hens, game birds, rabbits, hares, pigs and boars. The numbers ranged from 7,000 hens to 70 boars. An extra 100 boars were ordered in November. The bread was ordered locally in November, no less than 68,500 loaves at a cost of over £7,000. These loaves were reckoned at four to the penny, so were not very large. The fish were ordered in December and included herring (60,000, probably salted), greenfish (1,000, probably unsalted cod), haddock (10,000) and conger eels (500). Fresh-water fish from the King's stew pond on the River Foss were also ordered, to be stored live until required. The wine (100 tuns, about 25,000 gallons) was ordered in early August and the rice, almonds and sugar at the end of November. The wardens of Galtres and Langwith Forests were ordered in November to allow the collection of the large amounts of wood and charcoal needed as fuel to cook all this food. It is clear that the royal household must have had a tried and tested routine (and indeed timetable) ready to go into operation when needed on these occasions.[2]

There also exist menus for many feasts, and lists of the quantity of food that was bought for each occasion. A number of existing recipe books also frequently include menus. The recipes were not necessarily used for particular feasts, but are a good indication of the kind of food that was prepared for them. They mostly date from the early fourteenth century onwards, although there is evidence that many of the recipes described in them date from considerably earlier than this. For example, references in a tweflth-century manuscript mention dishes that are fully described in later manuscripts.[3] The recipes do not give precise instructions, nor any indication of quantity, so quite how they were used is a mystery. For example, they specify taking a whole swan, to season something well, or to 'boil for a while'. They were presumably intended for those in charge, rather than for use by the ordinary cook in the kitchen, most if not all of whom probably worked (as do many nowadays) by memory, experience and training. It may be that a menu was chosen first, and then recipes were used to estimate the amount of ingredients that would be needed.

Whoever the recipes were intended for, it appears that the English instructions were initially, sometimes at least, much less detailed than the French versions of the same dish. In one case it almost looks as though the English recipe was intended for cooks who knew the basic dish but needed help in preparing the sauce that went with it. The spices were specified with a fine discrimination in a way that the French version does not. This occurred with other dishes too. These brief and often cryptic versions of recipes in the English manuscripts slowly changed with time, as more and more detail was added. Dishes also changed in nature. In the case of 'Mawmenny', for example, which dates from Anglo-Norman times, this was originally a dish containing ground beef, pork or mutton boiled in wine, served in a wine-based sauce which was thickened with capon meat and almonds. The sauce was seasoned with cloves and sugar, fried almonds were added and the dish coloured with indigo or with a red dye. About sixty years later it had changed into a dish made from beef broth (no wine), capons cooked in milk of almonds and the whole thickened with rice flour or breadcrumbs. It was seasoned with somewhat stronger spices and coloured yellow with saffron. After another fifty years the wine had returned, together with a great deal more sugar, the beef had vanished but the capon remained. There were more spices, the almonds had been replaced by pine nuts and dates, and the colour was now a reddish orange. This was part of a process in which it appears that, as time went by, a dish tended to become sweeter, spicier and more complicated. For example, more dried fruit was added by the fifteenth century. John Russell in his *Boke of Nurture* (of *c.* 1430) complained of new and more complicated cookery, and 'cookes with theire newe conceytes, choppynge, stampynge and gryndynge'.[4]

The recipe for mawmenny rather neatly summarizes the prevailing impression given by medieval food. It utilized very large numbers of ingredients – meat, fish, fowl and vegetables – in amazing variety. The overwhelming impression is of complication, the use of colour and of the high cost. The great ambition of the medieval cook was to disguise nature, and to turn a fairly bland original into something exotic and piquant. To this end he was prepared to use a great many things and in greater quantities than we would, of which spices are perhaps the most noticeable. These were used in great variety, not necessarily in great quantity, although this is disputed. In some instances the amount used over a year does not seem to be excessive (see the de Bryene household in Chapter 4), although in others it does (for example, ½ lb of ground cinnamon and 1 lb of ginger among many others for a wedding party with forty guests).[5] It is impossible in any case to know how much spice was used in any one dish, since the recipes rarely gave quantities for any ingredients, and certainly not for the spices. The outstanding point is the number of different spices put into any one dish. Mixtures such as pepper, cloves, mace and cubebs; or ginger, cinnamon, galingale (a spice similar to ginger), cloves and sage, are not uncommon, sometimes with the addition of sugar to take the edge off the spices. Sometimes ready-made mixtures of spices were used: 'powdour marchant', 'powdour douce' (which was relatively mild, and usually contained sugar and cinnamon rather than pepper) and 'powdour fort'. The latter was the strongest and seems to have contained pepper, but their precise composition is not known.[6] The flavourings were undoubtedly stronger than those we are used to today, as with the cinnamon soup, served at a banquet in the early fifteenth century. This also applies to some of the meat eaten then. Whale, porpoise, seal, swan, crane, heron, peacock and seagull, were all eaten, each of which is strong tasting. These and many other slightly more flavoursome game birds, such as stints, redshanks and snipe, were listed in the Earl of Northumberland's household book, to be bought and served only at feasts and only to the Earl. 'Smale byrdys' also appear in the records of food eaten at feasts. These were probably larks, the favourite small bird, since 'feldefare' and thrushes are mentioned separately.[7]

Flavours were often mixed, with both salt and sugar

appearing in the same dish, much as sugar and spices did (as already noted, sugar was regarded as a spice). Much wine was used in cooking and appears in many recipes, as does ale (both sound and stale), vinegar and verjuice (the juice of crab-apple as well as of unripe grapes). A sauce made from wine, verjuice, powdered ginger and salt brought together several of these flavours and gives some indication of the flavours desired.[8]

As mentioned, there are many menus of medieval feasts in existence, so perhaps the best way to deal with the food served is to discuss just two of these in detail. All feasts took the same general pattern of two, three or four (occasionally more) courses, each consisting of several dishes. The more eminent the occasion, the more dishes per course. The order of the dishes within the course seems in some ways almost random, despite such authorities as Olivier de la Marche, the master of ceremonies to the protocol- conscious court of Burgundy. De la Marche said that soup was served at the beginning, then the eggs, fish and meats, then the *entremets* (a cross between side dishes and entertainments), such as swans, peacocks or pheasants dressed in their plumage, and finally the dessert. However, the fifteenth-century *Modus Cenandi*, while agreeing that soup came first, suggested that flesh dishes (both animals and birds) followed, then pies and pasties, then fried dishes, and finally the dessert, wafers, fruits, light cakes and (probably) spiced wine. On fast days soup was to be followed by fish dishes, then 'soft dishes' and lastly fried puddings. Another fifteenth-century manuscript gives an elaborate order for a fish course, with salted fish followed by fried fish, then sea fish, fresh-water fish, roast fish and so on. This seems more like an intellectual exercise than a practical suggestion, however. To some extent all menus seem to follow a general rule: soup or something like it to begin with, followed by more substantial dishes, including roasts, small pies or pasties, then lighter and/or richer dishes, such as tarts and fritters, then something sweet.[9] This order was only followed approximately, however. Probably the main consideration was convenience. Most of the 'made' dishes seem to have been designed to eat with a spoon, as the ingredients were cut or pounded up small.

A relatively modest feast was that described by the *Ménagier* of Paris. The *Ménagier* gave the arrangements and menu for a wedding feast on a Tuesday in May, arranged for one Jean du Chesne. Du Chesne was apparently someone of similar status to the *Ménagier*: a fairly wealthy townsman, and possibly a merchant. The *Ménagier* not only gave the menus for the dinner and supper, but also set out the ingredients that would have been needed, together with the shops or markets where they were to be bought, the quantity required, the price and everything else that would be needed. The venue was the hotel of the Bishop of Beauvais, which was hired out to M. du Chesne. This was often done when the owner was not in residence. The tables, trestles and benches came from the same source. The feast was of twenty covers (and, since a cover in this sense meant a mess of two, was thus for forty people). The food followed the usual pattern of meat, pottage and roasts, followed by entremets (see below), desserts, hippocras and wafers (or fruit and cheese in the summer), and the 'sally forth' (*boutehors*), which consisted of spiced wine and spiced sweetmeats, intended to aid the digestion. The latter were served after the guests had washed their hands and heard grace.[10]

The feast was not as elaborate as the number of diners and courses makes it sound. There was only one soup (of ground capon thickened with almond milk and served with pomegranates and red comfits), and the roast dish consisted of kid (better than lamb according to the *Ménagier*), duckling and spring chickens, all served on the same dish. The entremets were crayfish set in jelly, loach fish, and young rabbits and pigs. The dessert was 'frumenty' (or 'furmenty', a kind of wheat porridge with eggs and milk) with, in this case, venison. A supper of ten covers, presumably after the wedding, with slightly more elaborate dishes, included a pasty of two young hares and two peacocks, and another dish of minced kid with the heads halved and glazed.[11] The organization and purchases that lay behind these meals were also described. The number of chickens and pigs to be bought were specified, together with how much and what kind of spices (no less than 1 lb of ginger, ½ lb of cinnamon and much sweet stuff: candied orange peel, rose (scented) sugar and white comfits), the weight of almonds (10 lb), the number of oranges (50), the buying of sauce (in this case 'cameline' sauce which usually contained cinnamon). The eggs (300) went partly with the six green (fresh) cheeses, since the *Ménagier* noted that each cheese should make six tartlets and three eggs were allowed per cheese. For trenchers, 120 flat, white loaves and 36 coarse, brown loaves 'six inches wide and four inches high' were purchased. A quarter of veal was specified for making the blankmanger (a dish of meat minced with cream, almonds, eggs, etc.). This would have made a less rich stock than beef, and would thus have been more suitable for those of lower rank.[12]

The number of candles needed amounted to 2 lb, plus six 3 lb torches and six flambeaux. The latter could be sold back to the dealer at a little less than was paid for them, to take into account the amount used. This was probably not a point that would worry the ranks above the Goodman. Some of the necessities, the sauces and the hippocras (3 quarts) were bought ready-made. There was coal to buy, branches of greenery to decorate the hall, and violets and green herbs to strew on the floor. Someone had to make the wedding garlands, and find the salt cellars for the high table, 48 'hanaps' (ornate goblets), 4 covered gilt goblets, 6 ewers, 48 silver spoons, 4 silver quart pots, 2 comfit dishes and 2 alms dishes (for putting the scraps and leftovers in to give to the poor). Some of these were probably borrowed (but not hired, since they are not mentioned in the list of wedding expenses), and it seems unlikely that a rich bourgeois would have this large number of spoons when the King of France at this time had only 66 himself.[13] Staff were also needed to attend to the guests. Some of them must have been provided from those in the household of the bride's father, but others, including the cook and his two helpers, were hired for the occasion. Equipment needed in the kitchen was hired. Two 'knife bearers' (*portechappes*) were hired to cut up the bread to make trenchers and salt cellars. Only those at the top end of the table had a 'salt', the others made do with a trencher with a piece cut out. The knife bearers also carried the bread and salt to the table. Stewards seated the guests and told them when to rise, and a sewer and two servants served and took away the food, throwing the remnants into baskets and buckets (for the liquids) provided by the *portechappes*. Esquires poured the wine and looked after the spoons, giving them out and collecting them in again.[14]

At the other end of the social scale was the feast at the coronation of Richard III in 1483. There were three courses of 15, 16 and 17 dishes, respectively. There is no reference in the 'ordynaunce' for the coronation banquet to a fourth course of wafers, fruit and spiced wine, which must have been planned as part of the normal procedure. However, we know that wafers and hippocras were provided instead of the third course, which was not served since it was too dark (that is after about 10.00 p.m. since it was summer). The third course must have been cooked, so one wonders who ate it. If it was the cooks and kitchen staff they probably deserved to do so.[15] The first course consisted of five meat, five dishes containing birds, one fish and four indeterminate dishes. The second included four meat, probably two fish, six of birds and three indeterminate dishes. The uneaten third course consisted of three meat, two fish, five of birds, two fruit, three indeterminate and one unidentifiable dish. This latter, 'nosewis in compost' (compost, that is *compote*, was a chutney-like preserve), shows the pitfalls in studying medieval cooking when the terms used are rarely defined and the meaning has to be determined from many sources.[16]

Not all of those present were given the opportunity to eat each of the dishes. Only those at the very top table were expected to have them all. In this particular coronation banquet the 'lordes and ladyes' were given a selection in two courses (with some additions not supplied to the top table), and the 'comons' had one course of three dishes. In some instances the amount of food supplied makes it clear that those lower down the table would not have seen some of the more exotic dishes. For example, the 36 egrets would not have gone far, even on the topmost table.[17] The dishes served in 1483 were very approximately in the order described above. The first course started with soup, although the second and third did not. Many of the dishes were roast meat of various kinds. Most of the bird dishes were roasted, and included several dishes of the exotic game birds without which no feast was complete, such as rail, bittern, crane, egret and young heron. Well-fatted capons in lemon and roast partridge were also listed. Other less exotic-sounding dishes included roast suckling rabbits and pigeons, rolls of stuffed venison (or possibly seasoned venison), beef and mutton (possibly stewed or roasted). Roast meats were nearly always served with a sauce, although some birds, such as egrets and curlews, were served only with salt. Sauces were regarded as an important part of a dish and were served separately. A sauce poured over a dish, or one in which it was served, was known as a 'sewe' (or cirip, or syrippe). Following these heavier meat dishes there were several made dishes such as a 'custard' (an open tart that sometimes contained a thick, egg-based filling, rather like a quiche), and a 'flampayne', another tart (possibly containing a pork mixture), decorated with pastry 'points', which was sometimes called 'flampoyntes'. Eggs were widely used very extensively in tarts and custards. Large numbers were bought for normal use, and on feast days the numbers sometimes reached the incredible. In Easter week in 1265 the household of the Countess of Leicester bought some 3,700 eggs (some of which may have been used as painted Easter eggs), and a feast given for Richard II in 1387 required 11,000.[18]

Several of the dishes served to Richard III were very typical of the period. For example, the soup with which the guests began was partly 'frumentie'. Sometimes known as 'furmenty', this consisted of boiled, hulled wheat and milk of almonds, rather like a porridge, to which was added a meat, in this case venison, and saffron or other spices. With this was served a broth ('bruet'), in this case 'of Tuscany' (the significance of this name is not known). 'Brewet of Almayn' was common and frequently contained rabbit, the ubiquitous almond milk, and spices such as ginger, cloves, nutmeg and galingale. Sometimes sugar, or onions, cloves and raisins were added.[19] The first course also included 'mamory' (mawmenny) described above. Another of the exotic dishes was 'blaundsorr' with which the third course started. This was a pottage based on almond milk, thickened with rice and containing ground capon, thus forming a kind of meaty (occasionally fishy) blancmange. There were no examples of the really exotic, such as pike cooked in three ways: boiled at the head, fried in the middle and roasted at the end. This was known as 'glazed pilgrim' and included roast lampreys or eel as the pilgrims' staffs. There were several jellies and 'frettours' (served towards the end of each course), hardly exotic perhaps but apparently very popular.

Some of the most interesting dishes were very typical of the time. For example, there was considerable use of exotic colouring, and one dish was specifically described as 'purpill'. This was probably a red colour, perhaps from 'saundres' (a variety of sandalwood much used for colouring), 'dragon's blood' (a bright red dye obtained from various plants) or even alkanet from the plant of that name.[20] The appearance of food was very important, and probably the majority of dishes were coloured in some way, often with saundres, or with saffron to give a bright yellow, as in frumenty and mawmenny above. A popular way to colour a dish was to 'endore' it, that is to paint it with egg yolks (or a mixture of eggs, ginger and saffron) and cook it to a golden crust. Green was obtained by using mint or parsley juice, and black or brown from blood or burnt breadcrumbs. Blood was also much used in sauces. With roast swan, for example, the entrails, ginger, pepper, cloves, wine and salt were used together with the blood, which would presumably have coloured it black. Some dishes were given several colours, perhaps quartered white, yellow, green and black, as in one complex fish dish.[21] Another practice, similar to colouring food, was to cover a dish in gold or silver foil. One dish in the third course was described as 'pety chek in bolyen' (that is small chicks in bullion, or gold foil). Other recipes are known in which this occurs. In one case a pig was stuffed with a cock, which was itself stuffed with a mixture of pine nuts and sugar, and the whole roasted. It was then coloured with eggs, saffron, and gold and silver foil. Another dish in the second course of Richard III's coronation banquet was described as 'gret carpe and breme in foile', but in this case it may have been in thin pastry, also known as foil. One dish is described as 'gely partied with a devise'. This may just refer to 'parting' with pastry, but in combination with 'devise' (a symbol of some kind), it may have been similar to the dish at the coronation of Henry VI where the 'gely' (jelly) was inscribed '*te deum laudamus*'. This could have been something of particular relevance to Richard III, chosen especially for the occasion: perhaps a heraldic 'devise' of some kind as also occurred in the coronation banquet of

Henry VI, which seems to have had particularly heraldic food. Similarly in a banquet given by the Count of Savoy for his father-in-law the Duke of Burgundy in 1403, 'parmesan pies' were served that had been gilded in a chequer pattern and banners set on top, painted with the arms of those before whom they were placed.[22]

Other particularly interesting dishes worth mentioning were the 'fesaunt in trayne' and the 'pecockes in his hakell and trapper', the *entremets*. These are examples of the practice whereby these birds were skinned with great care, before roasting, so as to keep the skin whole and complete with feathers: 'the skyn and the ffethurs togidre and the hede still to the skyn of the necke and kepe the skyn and the ffethurs hole togiders'. The neck was also left whole. When the cooking was complete, the bird was allowed to cool, the skin replaced and the bird presented as though still alive. The same was done with the pheasant, with the beautiful tail feathers in place. They must both have made very spectacular table decorations, although the risk of infection from the uncooked skins would have been great. Swans were treated similarly.[23]

As mentioned above, the third course of the 1483 coronation banquet was not served, but was replaced by what must have been part of a planned fourth course. The ordinance did not allow for this, although ingredients for a considerable number of wafers were included, together with 116 gallons of hippocras plus 63 gallons of wine from which to make it. From this it appears that most of the hippocras was bought in rather than made for the occasion. Wafers and hippocras were essential parts, and probably the only ones that always appeared of this last course, the 'voide', as it was usually called. As seen (in Chapter 5), it was served with considerable ceremony. Hippocras was a complicated mixture of red or white wine plus, according to one recipe, 3 oz of cinnamon, 3 oz of ginger, one penny's worth of spikenard of

Spain (a herb), ¼ oz each of galingale, cloves, long pepper (a variety of pepper thought to be a superior kind), nutmeg, marjoram and cardamom, and finally ½ oz each of grains of paradise and flour of cinnamon (probably just good-quality cinnamon). These spices were strained through bags according to a method of *c.* 1430. Sugar was not mentioned, although it was an important ingredient, and no volume is given for the amount of wine to be used, so this was probably a standard amount, such as a gallon. A less complicated mixture was apparently considered good enough for the 'commyn peple'.[24] Wafers could be savoury (with cheese or fish), spicy, or, in the case of those served after the meal, sweetened with sugar or honey. Other items sometimes served were fresh fruit (for example, apples and pears of many varieties, cherries and quinces), although these were regarded as difficult to digest and therefore better served, if at all, early in the meal. John Russell recommended serving plums, damsons, cherries and grapes before the first course, but he also apparently served them after as well. Nuts, cheese, comfits (for example ginger or dates in sugar), sugar candy, raisins and dates were also included.[25]

Other feasts of which records exist were very similar to that of Richard III. They mostly date from the fourteenth and fifteenth centuries, with isolated references to meals from the twelfth century and one from the late thirteenth. The latter is a description of an anonymous 'great banquet'. The succession of courses was not unlike that already described, and could have been served at any time between the thirteenth and the mid-sixteenth centuries without causing comment. These included roasts, rabbit in gravy covered in sugar, mawmenny and fritters. The same applies to the dishes known from the twelfth century. These courses included roast crane and peacock with pepper sauce. Some menus exist that were for feasts held on fast days and these include only fish dishes instead of a mixture of meat and fish.[26] Vegetables are rarely mentioned in menus. They do feature on occasion, as, for example, in a dish of peas and porpoise mentioned in one of John Russell's sample menus, and in extant recipes, but not as much as modern practice would require. Such dishes as rapes (turnips), or parsnips in pottage, which also included onions, saffron and spices, were made, as well as 'gourds' (probably marrows) in pottage (with onions, egg and pork) and 'caboches' (cabbage) with onions, leeks and spices in pottage. Beans, frequently ground, were also eaten in various combinations. All of these vegetables, together with radishes and carrots, were grown in medieval gardens. Herbs, too, were grown and put into dishes, apparently in quite large quantities. For example, a 'pottage of pot herbs' of *c.* 1390 contained borage, kale, langedebef (*langue de boeuf*, or bugloss), parsley, beet (probably leaves rather than the root), orach, avens, violets, savery and fennel in broth. One later (*c.* 1450) version of this specified beef broth, and added hare, but said that goose would do as well. Most dishes with herbs contained fewer than this 'pottage'. Mint and parsley were used fairly frequently, however. Salads, too, were eaten. One from the late fourteenth century contained a very wide range of herbs and vegetables, including common ones, such as onions, spring onions and cress, with less well-known vegetables, such as purslane, all presented in a familiar manner: 'pluk hem small with thyn honde and myng hem wel with rawe oile; lay on vynegar and salt and serve it forth'. Gilbert Kymer, a fifteenth-century writer on food, also said that vegetables were eaten raw in spring and summer, with olive oil and spices, although he disapproved of the custom.[27] It is usually said that vegetables, as such, were despised in the Middle Ages, since these were what the peasants ate. This is undoubtedly true, and Harrison, in the mid-sixteenth century, agreed, but they were still eaten by all classes. In 1482 John Howard, Duke of Norfolk, bought 'erbes for a selad', so the prejudice was obviously not too extreme. To some extent herbs were treated as vegetables, all going under the general name of 'wort', but it seems fairly clear that herbs must have been distinguished in use since they were often included in recipes for their fragrance rather than their nutritional value. In the same way flowers were used as decoration, as the violets may have been in the 'pottage of pot herbs' mentioned above, although boiled and ground violet petals were also used to colour such pale foods as milk puddings. Roses, primroses and hawthorn flowers were used in the same way.[28] On special occasions, flowers, greenery and chaplets for the guests were incorporated into decorations, but neither these nor the 'device' mentioned above, nor even the pheasants in their original feathers, were the most spectacular table decorations used. These were the subtelties.[29]

A subtelty ('sotelty') was a table decoration introduced at the end of each course. Sometimes it was an ornament wholly made of sugar or 'marchpane' (marzipan) that was eaten. They were not, however, always restricted to edible materials – the cook probably used whatever was necessary to make his design. The object of the exercise was to impress the guests with the skill of the cook, and, naturally, with the equal cleverness of the host in employing him. Anything could be represented. In great feasts there was frequently a theme relevant to the occasion. For example, at the banquet after the coronation of Katherine, wife of Henry V, the three sotelties were all allusions to the circumstances of the occasion. Thus the first was of a pelican on its nest (an emblem of piety) and St Katherine disputing with heathen clerks (St Katherine was the patroness of learning), the second had an image of St Katherine with a wheel in her hand (she was martyred on a wheel) and the third showed a heraldic tiger looking in a mirror, with a man riding away carrying a tiger's whelp and throwing down mirrors behind him. In medieval legend the tiger could not resist looking in a mirror, thus to give her one was the only way to rob her of her young – an allusion to the marriage.[30]

The coronation banquet of Henry VI showed another use for the sotelty, as a political message. Under the terms of the treaty of Troyes, when Henry succeeded his father Henry V he became King of France as well as of England. By the time Henry was crowned at the age of eight in 1429 (he succeeded his father when he was nine months old), this claim was a lost cause, but the sotelties only reflect the claim. The first showed Henry between Saints Edward and Louis to symbolize his ancestry and claim to both thrones; the second showed Henry between his father and the Emperor Sigismund (who had supported the claim of Henry V); the third showed Our Lady sitting with the Child in her lap and holding a crown. Saints George and Denis (for France) were presenting Henry VI to Our Lady. With each of these was a short verse by the poet John Lydgate explaining the meaning of the tableau – that Henry VI was King of France by both descent and title – in case the meaning was unclear. There usually was such an explanation (although not by such an eminent poet), or a 'word' to amplify the meaning. These are known in instances where the recorder of the occasion was supplied with it. This system broke down after the coronation banquet of Elizabeth of York, wife of Henry VII, when the herald who documented the event merely noted that there was 'a soteltie, with writing of balads, whiche as yet I have not'.[31] At less important feasts the sotelties were not of such elaborate designs. Russell, in his *Boke of Nurture*, has two suggestions for subjects. One was a series showing the seasons as the four ages of man, while the other was a religious series of the Annunciation, the Shepherds and the Three Kings. However these were hardly simple. Perhaps many were more like the eagle, or the *agnus dei*, at the inaugural feast of John Chaundler as Bishop of Salisbury in 1417. Not all feasts had 'themed' sotelties. A banquet given by Cardinal Wolsey in 1527 for a French embassy had some that were very splendid, but which lacked any real coherence in design. A complete description of one from 1443, used at the installation of John Stafford as Archbishop of Canterbury, indicates the immense detail that some included. This soltelty showed 'a godhede in a son [sun] of gold glorified above; in the son the holy giste voluptable. Seint Thomas kneling afor him with the poynt of a swerd in his hede and a mitre theruppon, crowning Saint Thomas on the right hand side, Mary holding the mitre. On the left hand side John the Baptist and in the four corners four angels with censors'.[32]

Such feasts as that just described were not wholly devoted to eating, drinking and admiring the decorations on the table. An important part of the proceedings was the entertainment. Trumpets were played before each of the courses and to signal the beginning and end of the feast, and music was usually played during the meal, by the minstrels of the household, those of another household or minstrels attracted by notice of the feast. All large households, and probably many smaller ones, kept at least one minstrel on the permanent staff, even if they also had other duties, as even some of the royal minstrels of Edward I did. The minstrels of the greater households seem to have moved about and played before other households fairly frequently, presumably by arrangement. They appear to have been made welcome, perhaps because the lord of each household knew them personally. Minstrels were also taken with their lord to important occasions. Thus at the great feast given by Edward I at the knighting of his son, Edward, in 1306, there were many minstrels present who had been brought by the guests, earls, barons, knights and at least one abbot. There were also two minstrels of the King of France, doubtless attracted by the probability of largesse. That this movement of minstrels went on throughout the Middle Ages is evident from records. For example, in 1484, the minstrels who played before Richard III were those of his mother, the Duchess of York, his wife and his son. In 1512 the Earl of Northumberland stated in his household regulations that visiting minstrels should receive 3s. 3d. (16p). He also had regular visits from the King's juggler.[33]

The records of the feast in 1306 also gave some idea of the very large numbers of 'minstrels' that would have been present on these occasions. Many of the entertainers present were classed as minstrels, whether their main duty was to play an instrument or to entertain the audience in other ways. Singers were popular. They sang carols (of which many existed, and still exist) as well as (in the earlier Middle Ages, at least) the 'chansons de geste'. These latter were tales of romance and chivalry.[34] Acrobats, tumblers, jugglers, conjurors, animal trainers and dancers were all part of the troop and the fool too, although we do not hear as much of him as we might like. Little has been documented on the performances themselves. The dancing is likely to have been of an acrobatic kind. As Henisch has pointed out, to the medieval mind the dances that Salome did before Herod were those of a tumbler and acrobat, and she is shown performing thus in many contemporary manuscripts. One 'minstrel' at the 1306 feast was Matilda Makejoy, a 'saltatrix' (an acrobatic dancer). She had danced before the Prince Edward when he was only thirteen years of age and was to dance before the two youngest sons of Edward I in 1310, so her act presumably was indeed such as to 'Makejoy'.[35] Matilda was not on the permanent pay roll of the royal household, but the minstrels proper certainly were even if in 1306 many (if not all) of them appear to have been 'part time' minstrels, for example being paid as waferers and sergeants-at-arms also. There were, in addition, what appear to have been gentleman minstrels – amateurs who presumably only played before members of the royal family or very great lords. Edward I had at least 27 royal minstrels, but Edward III had only 16, which was probably a more usual number. Edward IV allowed for 13 in his *Black Book*, but payments for up to 19 can be found and livery for no less than 47 minstrels was given out of the Great Wardrobe before the coronation of Richard III. The Earl of Northumberland had 3 minstrels in 1512. Collectively these performers played a great many instruments: the harp, which was still popular at court in the early fourteenth century, the psaltery, various bowed instruments, stringed instruments, such as the lute and the citole, and wind and percussion instruments. In 1350 Edward III had 5 players of trumpets, 1 of the citole, 5 of the pipes, 1 of the tabouret, 1 of the naker (nakers and tabourets were types of drum), 2 of the clarion and 1 fiddler. The Earl of Northumberland's three musicians were tabouret, lute and rebec players. The wind instruments, trumpets in particular, were frequently played before each course of a banquet, or to warn the household that a meal was about to be served. One of Edward I's trumpeters appears to have been Robert Parvus (or Robert the Little), King of Heralds.[36]

As well as playing, the minstrels would have accompanied singers or sung themselves. Sometimes there were readers of amusing or interesting books, as when Froissart read from his own work at the court of Gaston de Foix in 1388. There were also professional reciters of romances who accompanied themselves on the harp, as described in the romance of Merlin (from the thirteenth century).[37] Another entertainment which contained elements of much of the above was the 'disguising', when a group of strangely and richly clad people entered the hall and performed a dance or a song before leaving as mysteriously as they had come. There is evidence that kings themselves sometimes took part in such amusements in the medieval period, as they certainly did later. Mummers provided similar entertainment, and short plays were sometimes performed as 'interludes'. In the early fifteenth century John Lydgate was a prolific writer of these forms of entertainment. His pieces were largely written for the pleasure of the young King Henry VI and his mother, although it is probable that the not more than six-year-old boy king would not have found the serious verse very enjoyable. Dancing and singing by the guests seem to have become part of the events after a feast at an early point in the Middle Ages. For example, in 1285 both forms of entertainment occurred after a tournament in France, and by the sixteenth century, dancing by the guests after the eating was over, along with other entertainments, was common.[38]

Much of the spectacle at an important feast was very theatrical. An important part of the proceedings was the decoration of the banqueting hall with tapestries or painted walls. Sometimes, too, the feasts were given in temporary halls set up especially for the purpose. Pies burst open to reveal, perhaps, jugglers or jesters, and challenges were issued. For example, at the great feast given by Philip the Good, Duke of Burgundy, in 1453, it was proclaimed that the 'Knight of the Swan' would encounter all comers at a joust. To complete the similarity with the theatre, music and dramatic interludes frequently occurred.[39] Sometimes the occasion was used as an opportunity to swear important oaths, for example to fight the Turk, or as at the great feast already mentioned (of 1306), when the eldest son of Edward I was knighted, to fight a nearer foe. At some point during this feast, possibly between the two main courses (the time when there was frequently a spectacle of some kind), the King's minstrels brought into the hall and took before the King two swans, highly ornamented 'with golden nets' and apparently covered with green silk. The minstrels invited those present, particularly the new knights, to vow some deed of arms before these swans. Vows before birds of some kind (particularly swans) were not uncommon. The significance lay in the occasion and the oath taken, not in vowing before a bird. On this particular occasion, Edward I swore to avenge the insult to the Church which had been caused by the murder of John Comyn in the presence of Robert Bruce in front of the altar. After he had done this he vowed never to take up arms against Christians again, but to visit the Holy Land (and presumably fight the Turk). The other nobles present bound themselves by similar oaths. Such extravagant vows were common.[40]

A popular way to entertain was to enact a pageant of some kind, frequently historical, using elaborate moving structures. Cities, ships and mountains were all represented at times. Some of these were often very large and spectacular, as in 1389 at a ceremonial meal to celebrate the entry of Queen Isabella into Paris. On this occasion things went disastrously wrong. A tower on wheels representing Troy, accompanied by another representing an assault tower manned by Greeks, and a model ship manned by 100 soldiers were pushed into the hall and a mock battle was supposed to take place. However, there were so many people in the hall (participants and spectators), that the entry of these large objects caused almost total chaos. The pressure of people was so great that 'no man could stir', and a table at which many 'ladies and demosels' were sitting was overturned. To get fresh air it was neccessary to break open a door near the queen. All the tables had to be cleared hurriedly to make more room (partly to release the trapped noble ladies), and the banquet ended rather more quickly than expected. Wine and spices were served as a sign of this and the King and Queen left in haste. Not all moving entertainments were as large as that in Paris. For example, in 1403 a moving castle in Savoy was smaller in size but larger than a subtelty. It was mounted on a two-man litter and made very largely of meat, pea and bean pastes. It was decorated with a fountain gushing wine, and such dishes as a glazed piglet and a re-dressed swan. It was sufficiently large to contain three or four young men playing on various musical instruments and singing.[41]

Many of the most spectacular celebration banquets in the medieval and early modern period were those given at betrothals and marriages. One such series was given in 1503 at the betrothal and marriage ceremonies between Prince Arthur and Katherine of Aragon. They went on for several days and demonstrate the major spectacle that a feast (or, as in this case, a whole series of them) could be turned into. One of the events took place on Friday 19 November in Westminster Hall. This was hung with rich tapestries of Arras and contained a cupboard of seven shelves. The cupboard was filled with 'as goodly and riche treasure of plate as ever cowde lightly be seen, moch therof golde and all the remante being gilt' (that is no silver dishes). The plate was later described as 'great and massy pottes, flagons, standyng cuppis, goodly bollys [bowls] and peces', a splendid sight indeed. At this event three pageants (or disguisings) were displayed on some of the first pageant cars seen in England, although they were well known in France and Burgundy. These were a castle drawn into the hall by heraldic beasts, a ship on wheels 'in right goodly apparell, havyng her mastys, toppys, saylys, her taclyng and all other appurtenans necessary unto a semely vessel, as though it hade been sayling in the see', and a mountain containing 'viii goodly knightes with their baners spred and displaied'. Speeches were made from all of these, and dancers descended from the last. After the three pageants had been removed, the audience began to dance. During the dancing (basse dances, slow and stately), Prince Henry, brother to the groom and only ten years old, suddenly threw off his gown because it encumbered him and danced with his sister Margaret (twelve years old) dressed in his jacket. In the 'void' (the parting meal) after this a further set of cups was brought in. Those on the cupboard were not touched – a splendid example of conspicuous display. In the banquet held in the Parliamentary chamber at Westminster on the following Sunday (it rained on the Saturday, so nothing took place), another large cupboard was built, apparently even larger than before, extending from the closet door to the chimney of the Parliamentary chamber. The banquet consisted of six courses, each of seven dishes, the first course of 'flesshe' and the last of 'frute'. Finally wafers and hippocras were served. The affair began at 7.00 p.m. and lasted two hours. After the meal there were dances, and everyone went into Westminster Hall where they all watched an interlude followed by disguisings, dances by disguised nobles and ladies, and then a 'pageant' consisting of a lantern containing many 'disguysid' ladies. The lantern was so well lit that all of the ladies could be seen inside it. They all descended and danced, as did most of the audience. Finally the void of spices and wine were served. These splendid events were the culmination of the medieval feast, and foreshadowed the even more splendid entertainments of the later Tudor and Stuart courts.[42]

AFTERWORD

In the eleven years since writing this book a great deal of new work on mediaeval food has been published, both on mediaeval food generally and on specific subjects such as the etiquette of carving and the ceremonies around serving food to a great lord. In this Afterword the opportunity has been taken to highlight some of this new work. The new books used are listed in the bibliography at the end of this section.

WHERE FOOD CAME FROM

The question of where food came from, i.e. grown locally or at a distance or imported from abroad has been discussed at length with respect to the city of York. Food sources were much the same as those discussed above for the larger city of London. The various markets selling meat, bread and so on were regulated as tightly as were the London markets, and the sales of bread and ale were regulated by the Assize of Bread and Ale which were national laws. York too had strong craft guilds who kept a stern eye on who was entitled to follow their various crafts and the city had its own regulations, controlling its interests and indeed controlling the guilds. By the mid sixteenth century at least the city could impose its own view of what a guild should do. Thus in 1553 three searchers of the Butcher's Company were imprisoned by the Lord Mayor, one for selling bad meat and the other two for not reporting him. Since the searchers were the guild police, who were supposed to check the quality of the goods sold by their fellow members and enforce the regulations of both guilds and of the city, this was obviously not something to be tolerated. In fact another merchant, a baker, was imprisoned at about the same time for complaining (albeit in somewhat intemperate language) at a change to the guild regulations imposed on the guild by the city council.[1]

FOOD OF DIFFERENT CLASSES

Much more has been written on the food of what might be called the 'feasting' classes rather than the peasant or servant classes although some interesting material has been published on the contents of urban cess pits and the plant material preserved there which gives us a view of what some ordinary town dwellers ate. A particularly rich source of this type of material is the city of York, much of it due to the wet soil. Analysis shows largely the seed material that remains after food has passed through the body or which fell in to the pit accidentally. Considerable amounts of different grains are found as well as pips from fruit of very many kinds and a small amount of tough vegetable matter, chiefly leeks. Most of these finds would be from working class houses and so corroborate other evidence for what they ate.[2] An interesting point about lower class food was made by Scully, in that roasting meat is a very fuel inefficient way to cook, so that these people would naturally use a stew pot, probably filled with the vegetables and grains found later in their cess pits.

More attention has been paid to the higher ranks in society because there is simply more information about what they ate. A lot of their food came from their own land for example and there are many household accounts in existence showing this, although as time went on more households bought food from local markets, and even town dwellers may have kept pigs or chickens. The change of food procuring habits in the case of very large households may have been due to less movement from manor to manor thus making it easier for the market holders to estimate and meet demand.[3] With the increase in expenditure in buying from markets the proportion of income spent on food can be estimated. Thus Joan de Valence, Countess of Pembroke spent in 1294-96 about 25 per cent of her income on food and drink and it appears that other noble households spent this or more. These figures do not include the cost of staff needed to procure, prepare and serve the food who numbered at least 28 out of a total staff of 85.[4]

One item which did mark out the higher status households from the others was the use of spices and they bought very large quantities of many different kinds. It might be thought that street salesmen (chapmen) would not stock such things, or if they did that they would only have a small amount of the more common ones, such as pepper. However, one chapman (at least) in York had the kind of stock that would be expected, such as ribbons, caps, mirrors and so on but also stocked most of the spices used in cookery. As well as pepper he sold cloves, mace, ginger (of several types), cinnamon and saffron. He had a stock of large quantities of all of these and while he may well have had regular high status customers for most of them he would presumably have expected to sell some to his other, poorer customers too.[5]

Afterword

ADULTERATION AND NUTRITION

Much interest has been shown in the question of nutrition in the sense of choosing particular foods for their supposed qualities as indicated by the mediaeval doctrine of the humours. It has been suggested that the increasing popularity of this doctrine (described briefly above, p. 88) did in fact cause an alteration in the amounts of different foods eaten, lowering the amount of ale and bread, increasing the amount of meat and decreasing the amount of fish eaten. On the continent it appears that the properties of food were always central in the thinking of doctors who were firmly of the belief that different foods affected health in different ways. This belief was evidently also accepted in England since it was shared by the doctors surrounding Edward IV of England, (above, p.98). The sick were also catered for by the doctrine of humours and one of the best known French collections of recipes, that of Master Chiquart, had a separate section of dishes for the sick.[6]

TABLE MANNERS AND FEASTS

In the considerable interest shown recently in the manners and etiquette of the feast, the preparation of the food to be eaten there as well as the kitchens in which it was prepared have not been forgotten.

Since the brief description of a mediaeval kitchen given above, much new work has been done. Indeed one very high status kitchen, that of Henry VIII, has actually been used to produce meals like those that would have been cooked there in the sixteenth century. Brears has described the operation of such a kitchen from the point of view of someone who has actually operated one, and in the process gained a healthy respect for the organisation and manpower needed to operate a large royal kitchen at full efficiency day after day. He makes the point that very efficient ventilation was needed, and in fact obtained, from the chimney system.[7] Good ventilation is needed because cooking was carried out on large open fires and a good air flow was necessary to provide oxygen. Kitchens were obviously designed with this in mind.

Thus in the kitchens of the Dukes of Burgundy in Dijon six fireplaces were provided around three sides of the room with a wide chimney in the centre to provide a draught. Other practical needs were not neglected. Stone sinks were provided under a very large window which also allowed light in for the workers at large tables as well as for the washers up. Light would have been short most of the time in these large rooms and it must have taken skill indeed not only to see what they were doing but in the dim and smoky light to control the large fires well enough to cook dishes requiring only a gentle heat. Professional cooks would be well skilled in how it was possible to produce flames of different heat, by choosing an appropriate wood for example. They also had to ensure there was enough fuel to keep the fires going, as letting them go out for lack of fuel in the middle of preparations for a banquet was not an option for a cook. Another problem in these kitchens was that smoke can contaminate a delicately flavoured dish and ruin the taste. It is difficult to see how they could avoid this but if they did contaminate a dish there were procedures they could apply which were supposed to remove the bad flavour.[8]

The actual recipes which we find in mediaeval manuscripts are remarkably cryptic. They lack any idea of quantities, time taken and heat necessary. This is certainly because these recipes were not intended to teach someone how to cook and were probably intended to remind the cook of the ingredients needed for that particular dish. He would already know how to prepare basic dishes. Hence the books of recipes do not describe how to make ordinary dishes (how to make pastry for example) as the master cook knew such things. The books of recipes may in fact have been compiled for the master or mistress of the household, as they are usually far too clean to have ever been used in a kitchen.[9]

The times at which meals were taken is discussed above (pp.104–106), These must have been approximate before the fourteenth century but in the latter part of the 1400s more accurate timing was possible (certainly in England) with the spread of more accurate clocks. Events were even timed nearly by the minute in the fifteenth century, in one of the Courtesy books of about the mid century the Marshall of the Hall was expected to be able to calculate when a meal had been on the table for three quarters of an hour[10]. With the ability to time things more accurately the actual time at which meals were taken became more important. This ability explains how the household ordinances are able to specify that meals should take place at particular hours, as noted above (pp.104–5). Using household ordinances it is possible to set out a timetable of events, giving the times at which they were supposed to happen. For example, breakfasts (where they are mentioned) took place at 8.00 a.m. For this to happen the cooks were expected to rise at 4.00 a.m. This early rising was partly because dinner, the main and most elaborate meal of the day, became more elaborate and more time was needed to prepare it. Perhaps due to this it was sometimes taken later at midday or just after instead of at 11.00 a.m.[11]

While the meal was being cooked the elaborate organisation surrounding the laying of the table and the seating arrangements were begun. Even laying the table linen was an elaborate process. This is mentioned briefly below (p.106). Three linen cloths together covered the table down the floor, with one on the table board, a second from the inner edge to the floor on the outer side and the third from the outer edge to the floor on the inner side. This arrangement meant that the cloth would be tight against the lord's legs as he sat down and he could not easily put his legs under the table. To alleviate this, two 'estates' were made. These were six inch pleats in the cloth made by laying the hand on the table, inserting a rod about six inches away from the hand towards the table end, raising the cloth and folding the linen over the hand. This was repeated about eighteen inches away from the first fold towards the other end of the table thus forming two pleats which gave space for the lord's knees.[12]

The ceremony surrounding the actual meal was similarly elaborate and serving staff wore a kind of uniform, with towels used as badges of office, as well as for practical purposes. The butler, one of the senior servants, wore his round his neck similar to a priest's stole, but the carver had his hung over his left shoulder and knotted at the hip, while the sewer (the server) wore his over his right shoulder. The waiters wore theirs over their left shoulders. In fact the diners sometimes also had their napkins, folded lengthwise into four, over their left shoulder or over their left forearm, conveniently for use. The carver was a very important participant in the meal ceremony and his knowledge of how to carve the different joints of meat, birds and fish was very important and must have taken considerable time to learn. Each dish had to be cut up carefully in a prescribed manner, all inedible parts removed and the resulting pieces presented to the lord with the appropriate sauce or syrup poured over it. The different ways of cutting up each joint, fish and bird was described in the books of Courtesy and these methods have been illustrated.[13]

It seems very likely that not many, if any, middle ranking householders would comply with all of this elaborate code of manners, they might well not have had the staff in any case, but all gentry and wealthier merchants would know how they were supposed to behave and certainly attempt to do so. The world of the middle ages was not, in terms of table manners at least, the barbarous one depicted at times in films.

NOTES

1   Ian Kershaw, Bolton Priory (1973), pp. 38, 39; P.D.A. Harvey, *A Medieval Oxfordshire Village: Cuxham 1240–1400* (1962), pp. 46, 49, 50; Colin Richmond, *John Hopton, a Fifteenth Century Suffolk Gentleman* (1981), p. 79. A similar Norfolk manor at an earlier period was growing about twice as much barley as wheat with less oats and peas: F.G. Davenport, *The Economic Development of a Norfolk Manor 1086–1565* (1906), pp. 27–9.

2   W. Ashley, *The Bread of Our Forefathers* (1928). Ashley makes out a persuasive case for the prevalence of rye as the crop of the peasant.

3   Ernle, Lord, *English Farming, Past and Present* (1936), pp. 8–9; Georges Duby, *Rural Economy and Rural Life in the Medieval West* (1968), p. 344; C. Anne Wilson, *Food and Drink in Britain* (1984), p. 216. Wilson quotes a late edition of Thomas Tusser's *500 Pointes of Husbandrie* (1590), pointing out the drawbacks of sowing maslin.

4   H.S. Bennett, *Life on the English Manor* (1937), pp. 78, 80; Ernle, *English Farming*, p. 31; Dorothea Oschinsky, *Walter of Henley and other Treatises on Estate Management and Accounting* (1971), pp. 175–8, 327–9; R.H. Hilton, *Medieval Society* (1966), p. 108; *Palladius on Husbandry* (1873/1879), pp. 31, 181. This was a popular handbook of farming in the Middle Ages, although it actually described Italian practice of the fourth century.

5   Bennett, *English Manor*, pp. 86–7; R.D. Connor, *Weights and*

Notes

Measures of England (1987), p. 167, n. 20, and Ch. 8. Bennett states wrongly that the medieval bushel was 20 per cent less than the modern one; the actual figure is about 7 per cent, although the medieval bushel varied widely. It is usually reckoned to be about 60 lb now. See also Oschinsky, *Walter of Henley*, pp. 173 and n. 325, 418; Ernle, *English Farming*, pp. 97–8; Kershaw, *Bolton Priory*, pp. 40, 75–6; Davenport, *Norfolk Manor*, pp. 29–30, 31; Marjorie McIntosh, *Autonomy and Community: The Royal Manor of Havering, 1200–1500* (1986), p. 150. For grain yield in various parts of England in the thirteenth and fourteenth centuries, see Edward Miller and John Hatcher, *Medieval England: Rural Society and Economic Change 1086–1348* (1978), p. 216 and generally. For the Continent as well as England, see Duby, *Rural Economy*, pp. 99–101 and the references there.

6 H.A. Monckton, *A History of English Ale and Beer* (1966), pp. 11–22, 75–6, 95; Reginald Sharpe, *Calendar of the Letter Books of the City of London: Letter Book L*, (1900–1912), pp. 211–12 (this ordinance made at the request of the Brewers Company was mainly to prevent the use of hops, see Ch. 4); H.T. Riley, *Memorials of London and London Life* (1878), p. 245. The beer-making (including malting) process in the sixteenth century was described by Harrison: W. Harrison, *Description of England* Part I (1877), pp. 158–63.

7 Helena Graham, 'A Woman's Work . . .': Labour and Gender in the Late Medieval Countryside', in *Woman is a Worthy Wight, Women in English Society c.1200–1500* (1992), pp. 136–44; McIntosh, *Autonomy and Community*, p. 228; Wilson, *Food and Drink*, pp. 334–5.

8 Mary Harris, *The Account of the Great Household of Humphrey, First Duke of Buckingham, for the year 1452–53*, Camden Miscellany Vol. xxviii (1984), p. 37; Gervase Rosser, *Medieval Westminster, 1200–1540* (1989), p. 137.

9 J.E. Thorold Rogers, *A History of Agriculture and Prices in England*, Vol. 4 (1882), pp. 362–3, 652; Wilson, *Food and Drink*, pp. 393–4.

10 Harvey, *Cuxham*, Appx 6, pp. 174–5; Hilton, *Medieval Society*, p. 110; G.C. Homans, *English Villagers of the Thirteenth Century* (1942), pp. 42, 60.

11 Reay Tannahill, *Food in History* (1988), p. 172; Ernle, *English Farming*, pp. 14, 98; Bennett, *English Manor*, p. 78; Miller and Hatcher, *Medieval England*, pp. 217, 218–19.

12 Harrison, *Description of England*, p. 144

13 Bennett, *English Manor*, p. 92; John Webb (ed.), *A Roll of the Household Expenses of Richard de Swinfield, Bishop of Hereford during part of the Years 1289 and 1290* (1855), p. ccxxx; Chris Given-Wilson, *The English Nobility in the Late Middle Ages* (1987), p. 94; Oschinsky,*Walter of Henley*, p. 425.

14 L.F. Salzman, *English Trade in the Middle Ages* (1931), p. 417; Thorold Rogers, *Agriculture and Prices*, Vol. 1 (1866), p. 633; E.M. Carus-Wilson (ed.), *Overseas Trade of Bristol in the Later Middle Ages* (1937), pp. 234–5.

15 Salzman, *English Trade*, p. 419; H.S. Cobb (ed.), *Overseas Trade of London: Exchequer Customs Accounts 1480–81* (1990), pp. 46–50.

16 Salzman, *English Trade*, p. 422; Cobb, *Overseas Trade*, pp. 46–50.

17 Thorold Rogers, *Agriculture and Prices*, Vol. 1 (1866), pp. 147–9, 626–31, Vol. 4, pp. 658–63.

18 Cobb, *Overseas Trade*, pp. xli, 14, 32; Salzman, *English Trade*, pp. 411–12, 413; Thorold Rogers, *Agriculture and Prices*, Vol. 4, 1401–1582, p. 673.

19 Andre Simon, *The History of the Wine Trade in England*, Vol. 1 (1906), pp. 11, 12, 16, 155; *Expenses of Swinfield*, pp. xliv, xlv; Thorold Rogers, *Agriculture and Prices*, Vol. 1, p. 620, Vol. 4, p. 636; Teresa McLean, *Medieval English Gardens* (1981), pp. 256, 257.

20 Margery James, *Studies in the Medieval Wine Trade* (1971), pp. 10, 59, 94, 98, 116; J.L. Bolton, *The Medieval English Economy 1150–1500* (1985), p. 290. The figures for the fifteenth century are for non-sweet wines. Figures for comparable dates in Eileen Power and M.M. Postan, *Studies in English Trade in the Fifteenth Century* (1933), pp. 330–60, which include sweet wines as well, are slightly higher; Simon, *Wine Trade*, Vol. 2, pp. 160–1.

21 Simon, *Wine Trade*, p. 110, 131. The wine gallon is equal to 0.833 of an Imperial gallon.

22 Simon, *Wine Trade*, Vol. 1, pp. 162, 169, 195, 230, 340, 355,

Vol. 2, pp. 132, 134; Anne Sutton and P.W. Hammond, *The Coronation of Richard III*, (1983), p. 296.

23 Simon, *Wine Trade*, Vol. 1, pp. 299–300; Sharpe, *Letter Book C*, p. 112.

24 Simon, *Wine Trade*, pp. 300–1, 302.

25 Bennett, *English Manor*, pp. 93, 94; C. Pullein, *Rotherfield* (1928), p. 70.

26 Bennett, *English Manor*, p. 94; Harvey, *Cuxham*, p. 63.

27 Keeping of Dogs to Hunt, etc. Act XIII, 13 Richard II, (1390).

28 *Expenses of Swinfield*, pp. liv–lv, xlix–xlx (for hunting with the falcon), cxxi, clxvii, cxcvi, ccxxxii. See the text volume, 1854, for references to the results of hunting in the winter months; Wilson, *Food and Drink*, pp. 76–7, 82.

29 J.M. Steane, 'The Royal Fishponds of Medieval England', in *Medieval Fish, Fisheries and Fishponds in England* (1988), p. 49; C.J. Bond, 'Monastic Fisheries', in *Medieval Fish*, p.77; Mary Harris, *Coventry Leet Book*, Part III (1909), p. 696.

30 Bond, *Medieval Fish*, p. 76; A. Saul, 'The Herring Industry in Great Yarmouth, *c.* 1280–*c.* 1400', *Norfolk Archaeology*, 38, 1983, p. 33; R.B. Dobson, *Durham Priory, 1400–1450* (1973), p. 264.

31 Bond, *Medieval Fish*, p. 76; Wilson, *Food and Drink*, p. 33; Margaret Wade Labarge, *A Baronial Household of the Thirteenth Century* (1965), p. 79.

32 Bond, *Medieval Fish*, p. 77; C.C. Taylor, 'Problems and Possibilities', in *Medieval Fish*, p. 468.

33 Carus-Wilson, *Trade of Bristol*, pp. 215–16.

34 *Overseas Trade*, pp. xl, 19; Salzman, *English Trade*, pp. 364–7.

35 Bond, *Medieval Fish*, p. 79.

36 Taylor, *Medieval Fish*, pp. 465, 468; Bond, *Medieval Fish*, pp. 76–7, 78–9; D.M. Palliser, *Tudor York* (1979), p. 188.

37 S. Moorhouse, 'Medieval Fishponds: Some Thoughts', in *Medieval Fish*, pp. 479–80, 481; Bond, *Medieval Fish*, pp. 86, 92. Bond, *Medieval Fish*, pp. 84–92, is a thorough discussion of weirs in all their ramifications; pp. 79–83 are on fishing in marshes and lakelands.

38 R.A. Chambers and M. Gray, 'The Excavation of Fishponds', in *Medieval Fish*, pp. 115, 127–8; Bond, *Medieval Fish*, pp. 96–103, for plans of very elaborate monastic fishponds.

39   Bond, *Medieval Fish*, p. 93; Christopher Dyer, 'The Consumption of Freshwater Fish in Medieval England' in *Medieval Fish*, pp. 32, 33; Steane, *Medieval Fish*, p. 46; *Calendar of Liberate Rolls 1245–1251* (1937), p. 273, *Calendar of Liberate Rolls 1260–1267* (1961), p. 190.

CHAPTER TWO: FOOD OF THE COUNTRYMAN

1   R.H. Hilton, *A Medieval Society, the West Midlands at the End of the Thirteenth Century* (1966), p. 113.

2   See Christopher Dyer, *Standards of Living in the Middle Ages* (1989), pp. 110–18; Bennett, *English Manor*, pp. 87, 89, 95; Ernle, *English Farming*, p. 64. For the feeding of hens, see Webb, *Expenses of Swinfield*, p. xliii. For different calculations on the amounts of land needed to live on, see Miller and Hatcher, *Medieval England*, pp. 147–50. For children being given porridge, see William Langland, *The Vision of William Concerning Piers the Plowman*, Vol. 1, (1886), p. 234.

3   R.M. Lumiansky and David Mills (eds), *The Chester Mystery Cycle* (1974), pp. 129–30.

4   Langland, *Piers the Plowman*, Vol. 1, p. 220, lines 282–303, p. 234, lines 92–3. The language in the quotation has been modernized somewhat. The diet of the poor peasant is in Walter Skeat (ed.), *Pierce the Ploughmans Crede* (1867), p. 29, lines 762–3, 787.

5   Walter Skeat (ed.), Geoffrey Chaucer, *Complete Works*, Vol. 4 (1896), p. 271.

6   G.C. Homans, *English Villagers of the Thirteenth Century* (1942), pp. 145–6, 153; Bennett, *English Manor*, p. 253; Miller and Hatcher, *Medieval England*, pp. 148–9; Christopher Dyer, 'English Diet in the Later Middle Ages', in *Social Relations and Ideas* (1983), pp. 197–204, 208. See also Hilton, *Medieval Society*, pp. 111–13.

7   Andrew Borde, *A Compendyous Regyment or A Dietary of Helth* (1907), pp. 262–4; Constance Hieatt and Sharon Butler, *Curye on Inglysch*, (1985), pp. 98, 114; Rotha Clay, *Medieval Hospitals of England* (1909), p.169.

8   Bennett, *English Manor*, pp. 184–5, 235; Thomas Percy (ed.), *The Regulations and the Household of Henry Algernon Percy the*

Fifth Earl of Northumberland (1905), pp. 76–7, 79; Barbara Hanawalt, *The Ties That Bound: Peasant Families in Medieval England* (1986), p. 57.

9   Hanawalt, *Ties That Bound*, pp. 55, 151–2.

10 Bennett, *English Manor*, pp. 88–9; Kernshaw, *Bolton Priory*, pp. 56–7. For ploughmen's wages in about 1270, see Davenport, *Norfolk Manor*, p. 24. For a series of examples of reduction in liveries, see Miller and Hatcher, *Medieval England*, pp. 51–2.

11 Homans, *English Villagers*, p. 288.

12 Homans, *English Villagers*, pp. 261, 358; Bennett, *English Manor*, p. 235; McIntosh, *Autonomy and Community*, pp. 149–50; Nathaniel Hone, *The Manor and Manorial Records* (1906), pp. 106–7.

13 Homan, *English Villagers*, pp. 262, 270; Bennett, *English Manor*, p. 111. In the case of the villeins who protested about the size of the loaves they received, they were fined 40s. (£2), a large sum.

14 Hone, *Manor and Manorial Records*, p. 230.

15 Homans, *English Villagers*, p. 269; Dyer, *Social Relations*, p. 213.

16 Bennett, *English Manor*, pp. 94, 95, 232; Dyer, *Social Relations*, pp. 208–9. For a long quotation from the medieval poem *The Parlement of the thre Ages* describing a night poaching expedition, see Bennett, *English Manor*, pp. 271–3.

17 Hanawalt, *Ties that Bind*, p. 158; Dyer, *Social Relations*, p. 214. For the feeding of hens, see Webb, *Expenses of Swinfield*, p. xliii. For the general increase in prosperity after the Black Death, see Maurice Keen, *English Society in the Later Middle Ages 1348–1500* (1990), pp. 64–9.

18 Homans, *English Villagers*, pp. 172–3; Bennett, *English Manor*, pp. 264–7; Hone, *Manor Records*, p. 95; Judith Bennett, 'Conviviality and Charity in Medieval and Early Modern England', *Past and Present*, 134 (1992), pp. 19–41; Hanawalt, *Ties that Band*, p. 59.

CHAPTER THREE: FOOD OF THE TOWN DWELLER

1   Galloway and Margaret Murphy, *London Journal*, 16 (1991), p. 3. See also Duby, *Rural Economy*, p. 128; Stephen Mennell, *All Manners of Food* (1985), p. 48.

2   Wilson, *Food and Drink*, p. 74; Tannahill, *Food in History*, pp. 171–2.

3   Galloway and Murphy, *London Journal*, p. 9; McIntosh, *Autonomy and Community*, p. 141 (by 1596, Essex cheeses always weighed 336 lb); Riley, *Memorials of London*, p. 228; Riley (ed.), *Liber Albus (Munimenta Gildhallae Londoninensis)*, Vol. 1 (1859), p. lxxxiv; Sharpe, *Letter Book F*, pp. 132–3; J.C. Drummond and Anne Wilbraham, *The Englishman's Food* (1958), p. 73; John Stow, *A Survey of London*, Vol. 1 (1908), p. 126.

4   Galloway and Murphy, *London Journal*, pp. 6–8; Riley, *Liber Albus*, Vol. 1, p. lxxxiv; Rosser, *Medieval Westminster*, pp. 135–7; McClean, *Medieval English Gardens*, p. 213.

5   Eileen Power (ed., trs.), *The Goodman of Paris* (1928), pp. 195–204, and see also pp. 24–5 for a list of herbs grown in gardens in the fifteenth century; Harvey, *Cuxham*, p. 39; Marjorie McIntosh, *A Community Transformed: the Manor and Liberty of Havering, 1500–1620* (1991), pp. 122–3; Alicia Amherst, 'A Fifteenth Century Treatise on Gardening by Mayster Ion Gardener', *Archaeologia*, 54 (1894), pp. 157–72; McClean, *Medieval English Gardens*, pp. 239–40.

6   Riley, *Liber Albus*, Vol. 1, p. 263; Ian Archer, *Hugh Alley's Caveat: The Markets of London in 1598* (1988), p. 5; Sharpe, *Letter Book G*, p. 266. Riley's *Liber Albus* contains many regulations relating to the sale of food in the City of London. The various parts were written in the fourteenth century.

7   Archer, *Hugh Alley's Caveat*, pp. 7–11.

8   Archer, *Hugh Alley's Caveat*, pp. 87–9; Heather Swanson, *Medieval Artisans: an Urban Class in Late Medieval England* (1989), pp. 11, 17; Riley, *Memorials of London*, pp. 180, 220–1; Sharpe, *Letter Book G*, p. 123; Riley, *Memorials of London*, p. 180. A description of a sixteenth-century provincial market is given in McIntosh, *Community Transformed*, pp. 146–53, and of the keeping of official weights and measures in Mrs J.R. Green, *Town Life in the Fifteenth Century*, Vol. 2 (1894), pp. 27–8.

9   Sharpe, *Letter Book G*, pp. xxvii–xxviii; J.S. Farley, *Town Life in the Fourteenth Century as seen in the Court Rolls of Winchester City* (1942), pp. 66, 70–1, 136.

10   Sharpe, *Letter Book E*, p. 131; Sharpe, *Letter Book G*, p. 139;

Notes

John Stow, *A Survey of London*, Vol. 1 (1908), p. 20; Drummond and Wilbraham, *Englishman's Food*, pp. 39–40; Riley, *Memorials of London*, pp. 458, 468; Archer, *Hugh Alley's Caveat*, p. 9.

11 Riley, *Liber Albus*, p. lxvii–lxviii; Sharpe, *Letter Book A*, p. 215; Sharpe, *Letter Book G*, p. 123.

12 Riley, *Memorials of London*, p. 644; Riley, *Munimenta Gildhallae Londoninensis*, Vol. 3, p. 365; Drummond and Wilbraham, *Englishman's Food*, p. 43.

13 Assisa Panis et Cervisae, 51 Henry III, statute 1; Sharpe, *Letter Book H*, p. 183; Farley, *Town Life in Winchester*, pp. 76, 79, 140, 141; Wilson, *Food and Drink*, pp. 218–19; Swanson, *Medieval Artisans*, p. 12.

14 S.J. Thrupp, *The Merchant Class of Medieval London* (1948), pp. 130–1; L.F. Salzman, *English Life in the Middle Ages* (1927), pp. 243–4; Derek Keene, 'Shops and Shopping in Medieval London', *Medieval Art, Architecture and Archaeology in London* (1990), pp. 34–8.

15 Keene, *Medieval Art*, p. 38; McIntosh, *Autonomy and Community*, pp. 153, 229; Riley, *Memorials of London*, pp. 426, 581–2; Riley, *Liber Albus*, pp. lv, lvii; Riley, *Liber Custumarum (Munimenta Gildhallae Londoninensis)*, Vol. 2, Part 1 (1860), pp. xxxii–xxxiii; Sharpe, *Letter Book H*, p. 214; Sharpe, *Letter Book I*, p. 151; Sharpe, *Letter Book L*, p. 310; For doubtless libellous comments on the hygiene in one cookshop, see G. Chaucer, 'Cook's Tale', *Complete Works* (1894), pp. 126–7.

16 Eleanor Hammond, 'London Lickpenny', *Anglia*, 20 (1898), pp. 414, 416. This poem was previously ascribed to John Lydgate but is not now thought to be by him. The 'grayns' in the penultimate line are grains of paradise, a spice; the 'flowre of rise' is rice flour.

17 P. Clark, *The English Alehouse: a Social History, 1200–1830* (1983), p. 11; Rosser, *Medieval Westminster*, pp. 130–1.

18 Act to avoid the excessive prices of wine, 7 & 8 Edward VI, *cap. v* (1553); Anne Crawford, *The Household Books of John Howard, Duke of Norfolk* (1992), Vol. I, p. 251; Swanson, *Medieval Artisans*, p. 23 (noting that hostels and inns in York were obliged to have a 'signe' over their door); Simon, *Wine Trade*, p. 152; Riley, *Memorials of London*, p. 387, see also Riley, *Liber Albus*, Vol. 1, pp. lxv, 453.

19 Sharpe, *Letter Book F*, p. 28; Sharpe, *Letter Book H*, p. 214; Sharpe, *Letter Book I*, pp. 236–7; Clarke, *English Alehouse*, pp. 22–3, 24; Harrison, *Description of England*, p. 295.

20 Riley, *Memorials of London*, pp. 223–4; For other efforts to keep public water supplies clean, see G.T. Salusbury, *Street Life in Medieval England* (1948), pp. 108–16, and Madeleine Cosman, *Fabulous Feasts; Medieval Cookery and Ceremony* (1976), pp. 93–6, 98–101.

21 In 1352 an Italian was granted a licence to sell red, white and sweet wines in the same tavern, 'notwithstanding the custom to the contrary', provided they were kept in separate cellars, see Sharpe, *Letter Book G*, p. 5.

22 'An Act to avoid the excessive prices of wine', 7 Edward VI, *cap.* 5 (1553). The sons of peers were exempt from this act; Sharpe, *Letter Book H*, p.368

23 Simon, *Wine Trade*, pp. 261–3; Power, *Goodman of Paris*, pp. 216–17. It has been suggested that wines in the Middle Ages would have been regarded as very weak by modern standards at about 8%. See S. Ordish, *Wine Growing in England* (1953), p. 21.

24 Webb, *Expenses of Swinfield* (1855), pp. xlv, ccxxix, (1854), pp. 32, 56, 96; Simon, *Wine Trade*, Vol. 1, p. 353, Vol. 2, pp. 165–6.

25 Simon, *Wine Trade*, Vol. 1, pp. 264–7, Vol. 2, p. 162.

26 Simon, *Wine Trade*, Vol. 1, pp. 268, 272–3, Vol. 2, pp. 163–4.

27 Simon, *Wine Trade*, Vol. 2, pp. 205, 206–8, 210–11.

28 Sharpe, *Letter Book F*, pp. 245–6; Sharpe, *Letter Book G*, p. 124; Riley, *Memorials of London*, p. 670; Sharpe, *Letter Book H*, p. 365. The Duke Of Clarence used 'osey' in his household in 1469 as well as 'malvesie', 'romenay' and 'bastard muscadelle': Society of Antiquaries, *A Collection of Ordinances and Regulations for the Royal Household* (1790), p. 101. Other wines, as well as those described, were imported, for example one called 'Tyre', which probably came from Italy near the Tyrrhenean Sea, and 'vin cuit', possibly from Italy. 'Muscadell', a sweet wine, came from Crete, Italy, southern France and Spain. There were others even more obscure, such as 'Campelyte' and 'Tente': Simon, *Wine Trade*, Vol. 1, pp. 290–1, Vol. 2, pp. 240–3.

29   Simon, *Wine Trade*, Vol. 2, pp. 244–52; Wilson, *Food and Drink*, p. 340; Hieatt and Butler, *Curye on Inglysch*, pp. 142–3, 148, 149–50, 386; C. Innes (ed.), *Ledger of Andrew Halyburton* (1867), p. lxxiv.

30   Sharpe, *Letter Book E*, p. 64.

31   Georgine E. Brereton and Janet M. Ferrier (eds), *Le Ménagier de Paris* (1981), pp. xxii–xxiii.

32   Power, *Goodman of Paris*, p. 34; Brereton and Ferrier, *Ménagier de Paris*, pp. l, lii, 221, 226.

33   The Diet and Apparel of Servants, 37 Edward III, *cap. viii* (1363); Dyer, *Standards of Living*, p. 210; Drummond and Wilbraham, *Englishman's Food*, p. 55; Harrison, *Description of England*, p. 150.

34   Drummond and Wilbraham, *Englishman's Food*, p. 56, quoting Frederic Eden, *The State of the Poor* (1797); Clay, *Medieval Hospitals*, pp. 167–8.

CHAPTER FOUR: FOOD OF THE GENTRY

1   K.L. Wood-Legh, *A Small Household of the XVth Century* (1956), pp. xviii, xxii–xxviii. For use of lemons, see Webb, *Expenses of Swinfield*, p. l. For stock of salt, see Anthony Bridbury, *England and the Salt Trade in the Later Middle Ages* (1955), p. 112.

2   Wood-Legh, *Small Household*, p. xxv; Webb, *Expenses of Swinfield*, pp. cxx–cxxi. The size of the sextary is not entirely certain, as is the case with most medieval measures. Some sources give an equivalent that would mean that the bishop and his guests received only about twelve pints on this occasion, a very low

3   Wood-Legh, *Small Household*, pp. xxviii, xxx, 9.

4   M.K. Dale and V.B. Redstone (eds), *The Household Book of Dame Alice de Bryene of Acton Hall, Suffolk, Sept. 1412–Sept. 1413*, (1931).

5   For further comments on this point, see Kate Mertes, *The English Noble Household, 1250–1600* (1988), pp. 11–113.

6   Dale and Redstone, *Dame Alice de Bryene*, p. 135; Percy, *Northumberland Household*, pp. 107–8.

7   Power, *Goodman of Paris*, p. 273. For 'muxlys', 'welkes' and

'schrympys', see Dale and Redstone, *Dame Alice de Bryene*, pp. 52, 74.

8 Dale and Redstone, *Dame Alice de Bryene*, p. 118

9 Dale and Redstone, *Dame Alice de Bryene*, pp. 132, 134. For slaughter dates for cows, Dale and Redstone, *Dame Alice de Bryene*, p.129. For use of salt, Bridbury, *Salt Trade*, pp. xv–xvi.

10 Webb, *Expenses of Swinfield*, pp. xxx, cvii.

11 Mertes, *English Noble Household*, p. 99. For missing cow, see Dale and Redstone, *Dame Alice de Bryene*, p. 129, for coney skins, p. 139, for missing capons, p. 134. See also Dyer, *Standards of Living*, p. 58–9.

12 Dale and Redstone, *Dame Alice de Bryene*, pp. 50, 103–4, 120, 126, 137; Harris, *Household of Buckingham*, p. 43; Webb, *Expenses of Swinfield* (1855), p. l; (1854), p. 64 (for salted greens: *viridibus salsis*).

13 The question of the number of loaves that could be made from a quarter of wheat is complicated. It has been calculated that a quarter of wheat should produce enough flour to make between 175 and 250 2 lb loaves. Walter of Henley said that Bishop Grosteste expected to make 180 loaves (brown and white) from a quarter of wheat, each weighing 2 lb, see Oschinsky, *Walter of Henley*, p. 405. The loaves of the household of the Duke of Clarence weighed about 1½ lb: Duke of Clarence, *Collection of Ordinances and Regulations*, p. 91.

14 Dyer, *Standards of Living*, pp. 58, 62; Dale and Redstone, *Dame Alice de Bryene*, p. 119; Percy, *Northumberland Household*, pp. 6, 134, 136–8, 180–1. From the reference to 'turnynge' it might be thought to be ale and not hopped beer that the earl drank, but there is no doubt that it was beer because the weight of hops used was given: this weight shows that it must have been less bitter than modern beer: Monckton, *Ale and Beer*, pp. 89–93. Monckton sets out the brewing details, and shows that mistakes were made in the volumes of ale shown made. Simon, *Wine Trade*, pp. 318–33 contains a most interesting list of wine prices from 1159 to 1390.

15 G.W. Kitchin (ed.), *Compotus Rolls of the Obedientaries of St Swithuns Priory, Winchester* (1892), pp. 343, 344 for references to two meals in the Lent period, pp. 342, 343 for figs and raisins. For Swinfield's Easter feast, *Expenses of Swinfield*, p. clxvii; Percy, *Northumberland*

Notes

Household, p. 12; Mrs Henry Cust, Gentlemen Errant (1909), pp. 8, 500–2. One of those who ate Barnacle geese on fast days was apparently the Duke of Clarence, see last reference.

16 Dale and Redstone, <i>Dame Alice de Bryene</i>, pp. 28, 58, 94.

17 Percy, <i>Northumberland Household</i>, pp. 57, 58; Harris, <i>Household of Buckingham</i>, p. 37 ; Dyer, <i>Standards of Living</i>, p. 57.

18 Percy, <i>Northumberland Household</i>, pp. 103–5, 112–14, 202–4. The deer were taken from a total of more than five thousand, pp. 409–10; Wilson, <i>Food and Drink</i>, p. 37 for eating puffins.

19 Percy, <i>Northumberland Household</i>, pp. 58, 75, 78; Dyer, <i>Standards of Living</i>, p. 57.

20 Percy, <i>Northumberland Household</i>, pp. 75, 80–2, 349–50; Society of Antiquaries, <i>Ordinances and Regulations</i>, pp. 171–3.

21 Dyer, <i>Standards of Living</i>, pp. 57, 65; Keen, <i>English Society</i>, p. 168.

22 Dyer, <i>Standards of Living</i>, pp. 55, 70.

CHAPTER FIVE: ADULTERATION AND NUTRITION

1 The Sale of Food Act of 1984, c.30, section 2(1). This quotation from a modern Act is oddly similar to the wording of a fourteenth-century Spanish law cited by F.A. Filby, <i>A History of Food Adulteration and Analysis</i> (1934), p. 221, from Travers Twiss (ed.), <i>Black Book of the Admiralty</i>, Vol. 3, Appx, Rolls Series (1875).

2 <i>Assisa Panis et Cervisiae</i>, 51 Henry III, <i>cap.1</i> (1266).

3 Simon, <i>Wine Trade</i>, Vol. 2, pp. 84–93.

4 Simon, <i>Wine Trade</i>, Vol. 2, pp. 66–9, 307, quoting Sharpe, <i>Letter Book F</i>; Riley, <i>Liber Albus</i>, Vol. 1, pp. lxi, 360; Sharpe, <i>Letter Book F</i>, p. 237; Sharpe, <i>Letter Book G</i>, p. 124; Monckton, <i>Ale and Beer</i>, pp. 56–7; 1 Richard III, <i>cap</i>. xiii, (1484).

5 Sharpe, <i>Letter Book L</i>, pp. 301–2; Riley, <i>Memorials of London</i>, p. 90. 'Foreign' bakers were those from outside the city and not necessarily from overseas.

6 Sharpe, <i>Letter Book D</i>, f. 189, cited by Filby, <i>Adulteration and Analysis</i>, p. 71, and see also pp. 73, 74–5; Riley, <i>Munimenta Gildhallae Londoninensis</i>, Vol. 1, pp. lxvii, 356, Vol. 3, pp. 415, 420, 426–8; Sharpe, <i>Letter Book H</i>, pp. 322–3.

7   Riley, *Liber Albus*, p. 707; Sharpe, *Letter Book F*, p. 246; Riley, *Memorials of London*, p. 213.

8   Riley, *Memorials of London*, pp. 318–9.

9   Riley, *Memorials of London*, pp. 670–2 (from Sharpe, *Letter Book I*); Sharpe, *Letter Book G*, p. 137.

10 Simon, *Wine Trade*, Vol. 2, pp. 253–4, quoting Peter Morwyng, *A New Booke of Destillayom of Waters, called the Treasure of Euonymous*, p. 405.

11 Riley, *Liber Albus*, Vol. 1, pp. 708–9; Filby, *Adulteration and Analysis*, p. 132. Several ordinances were issued against selling Gascon wine with other wine in the same tavern.

12 Simon, *Wine Trade*, Vol. 2, pp. 96–100; Margery James, *Studies in the Medieval Wine Trade* (1971), p. 162.

13 Riley, *Liber Albus*, pp. 316, 358–61; Monckton, *Ale and Beer*, pp. 53–4, 98.

14 Harrison, *Description of England*, Vol. 1, p. 161; J.S. Farley, *City Government of Winchester* (1923), p. 84; Riley, *Memorials of London*, p. 319.

15 Lumiansky and Mills, *Chester Mystery*, p. 351; Clark, *English Alehouse*, p. 100; McIntosh, *Autonomy and Community*, p. 228.

16 Clark, *English Alehouse*, pp. 31–2; Sharpe, *Letter Book H*, p. 365; Riley, *Memorials of London*, p. 666.

17 Filby, *Adulteration and Analysis*, p. 114; Sharpe, *Letter Book K*, p. 205; *Calendar of Patent Rolls, Henry VI, 1441–1446* (1908), pp. 184–5. Filby (and Drummond and Wilbraham, *Englishman's Food*, p. 44) both state, without giving a reference, that the City of London petitioned against the use of hops. If this is so, it would be odd in view of their action in 1418.

18 Sharpe, *Letter Book L*, pp. 52–3, 211–12, 295–7; *Victoria County History, Shropshire*, Vol. 2, (1973), p. 422; Borde, *Dyetary of Helth*, p. 256; Society of Antiquaries, *Ordinances and Regulations*, p. 218; Clark, *English Alehouse*, p. 97; An Act for Avoiding of Deceitful Buying and Spending corrupt and unwholsom Hops, 2 James I, *cap*. 18.

19 Against selling meat by candlelight: Riley, *Liber Albus*, Vol. 1, p. 714; Riley, *Memorials of London*, pp. 141–2, 426; Assize of Bread and wine, 51 Henry III, Statute 6, section 2 (*Statutes of the Realm, Temp. incert., Judic. Pillorie)*; putrid meat, fish, and poultry:

Notes

Riley, *Memorials of London*, pp. 139, 240–1, 328, 471–2; P.E. Jones, *Butchers of London* (1976), p. 140; regulations of the Cooks: Sharpe, *Letter Book L*, pp. 129, 311; selling fish: Wilson, *Food and Drink*, p. 38; W.N. Skeat (ed.), *Complete Works of Geoffrey Chaucer* (1894), p. 126. This cook was also accused of having a shop full of flies (*ibid*, p. 127).

20   Clay, *Medieval Hospitals*, pp. 168, 169.

21   Sharpe, *Letter Book D*, p. 196; Sharpe, *Letter Book H*, p. 400; Filby, *Adulteration and Analysis*, p. 27.

22   Filby, *Adulteration and Analysis*, pp. 26, quoting from the full Riley, *Letter Book E*, 44, 45; Bridbury, *Salt Trade*, p. 51, n. 2.

23   'A Diatorie' in Furnivall, *Babees Book*, pp. 54–9 (from about 1460); Borde, *Dyetary of Helth*, p. 246, (the quotation on sleeping after meals), 252–3, 254; Furnivall, *Babees Book*, pp. 252, 253, from William Vaughan, a later writer (1602). The *Dyetary of Helth* was first published in 1542. Borde also recommended that, when sleeping, one should wear a scarlet night cap, although whether this was the colour or the cloth is not clear. William Vaughan recommended that the night cap should have a hole in the top to let out vapour: *Babees Book*, p. 253; *Babees*, pp. 49–50 (from *Modus Cenandi*, a later manuscript); *Secretum Secretorum*, Vol. 1 (1977), pp. 350, 360. The *Secretum Secretorum* was a well-known work in Europe in the Middle Ages, dating from about the twelfth century, and itself a translation of an Arabic original dating from the ninth century. It is a treatise on how the ruler of a state should behave, including dietary hints.

24   Drummond and Wilbraham, *Englishman's Food*, pp. 71–2; Barbara Wheaton, *Savouring the Past* (1983), pp.17–18. For a useful discussion of the system of humours as applied to foods, see Drummond and Wilbraham, *Englishman's Food*, pp. 65–75.

25   Dyer, *Standards of Living*, pp. 199, 202; F.G. Emmison, *Tudor Secretary, Sir William Petre at Court and Home* (1961), p. 137. Dyer has also shown that the diet of harvest workers also contained much more meat by the fifteenth century, and considerably more ale with less bread, p. 158. For the increase in meat eating in Europe in general, see Massimo Livi-Bacci, *Population and Nutrition* (1991), p. 94, and for wages, p. 101.

26   'Articles devised by the King's Highness . . . for the

establishment of good order . . . in his most honourable household', etc.: Society of Antiquaries, *Ordinances and Regulations*, pp. 137–240. The diets are on pp. 174–92; For the diets in Percy's household, see *Northumberland Household*, pp. 73–95. A most useful series of 'diet' accounts from the late fourteenth century to 1466 has recently been published, C.M. Woolgar, *Household Accounts from Medieval England*, Part 1 (1992), Part 2 (1993).

27   Society of Antiquaries, *Ordinances and Regulations*, pp. 174–6; Mennell, *All Manners of Food*, p. 30; Percy, *Northumberland Household*, pp. 88, 90, 91 ff.

28   Society of Antiquaries, *Ordinances and Regulations*, p. 191; Emmison, *Tudor Secretary*, pp. 308–16. The Petre accounts date from the winter, which may account for the lack of fruit, although stored apples should have been available.

29   Hubert Hall, *Society in the Elizabethan Age* (1902), pp. 216, 217, 222, 223. Darrell's accounts are laid out meal by meal, but no quantities are given. There is no doubt that he would have had enough to eat in a nutritional sense.

30   Kitchin, *Compotus Rolls*, pp. 306–62.

31   Kitchin, *Compotus Rolls*, pp. 68, 321, 349. The monks (or the Prior at least) of Nostell Priory ate much the same things at about the same time (*c.* 1489–90):, Leeds Record Office, Nostell Priory C/1/1. I owe this information to Dr Charles Kightly, to whom I give my thanks. For the unbought milk, '*de manerio*', (ten gallons of it) used by the Countess of Leicester: T.H. Turner (ed.), *Manners and Household Expenses of England in the Thirteenth and Fifteenth Centuries* (1841), p. 37. Milk was also bought fairly frequently, two to three gallons or so at a time; Rosser, *Medieval Westminster*, p. 136.

32   Frederic C. Lane, 'Salaires et régimes alimentaires des marins vénitiens au début du xivth siècle', in *Pour une Histoire de l'Alimentation: Cahiers des Annales*, 28 (1970), pp. 79–84; Michael Prestwich, 'Victualling estimates for English garrisons in Scotland during the fourteenth century', *English Historical Review*, Vol. 82 (1967), pp. 536–43. There are in fact two estimates included in this article, one for 1300 and the other undated but of about the same time.

33   Approximate figures only are given for the calorie counts since

the quality of the food is not known in either case, nor are the actual weights known in the case of the British troops. The amount of beef for the English soldiers was a fortieth part of a carcass between eight men. If a carcass weighed 320 lb (see p. 19), this would give 1 lb of meat per man. The allowance of pork was less generous: one fiftieth part of a carcass. For the Arles clerics, see Mennell, *All Manners of Food*, p. 45.

34 C.S.L. Davies, 'Les rations alimentaires de l'armée et de la marine anglaises au XVIth siècle', in *Pour une Histoire*, pp. 93–5.

35 For an analysis of these maintenance agreements, see Dyer, *Social Relations*, pp. 197–207. As Dyer points out, these agreements were not necessarily kept, but they show what this group of 'pensioners' expected.

36 Margaret Chaney and Margaret Ross, *Nutrition* (1971), pp. 91, 114; Mennell, *All Manners of Food*, p. 46; Drummond and Wilbraham, *Englishman's Food*, p. 465. Livi-Bacci has collected together some useful information on caloric balance of (chiefly) the peasant population of medieval Europe, see pp. 79–85.

37 For vitamins in general, see A. Stewart Truswell, *ABC of Nutrition* (1986), pp. 57–63. See also A.A. Paul and D.A.T. Southgate, *McCance and Widdowson's The Composition of Foods* (1978) and M. Livi-Bacci, *Population and Nutrition: an Essay on European Demographic History* (1991), p. 28.

38 Dyer, *Social Relations*, p. 196 suggests that the average diet would have been deficient in vitamin A. Given the large amounts in herrings this seems unlikely for the richer part of the community at least. For the possible deficiency in the diet of peasants, see Drummond and Wilbraham, *Englishman's Food*, p. 78.

40 W.J. White, *Skeletal Remains from the Cemetary of St. Nicholas Shambles, City of London* (1988), pp. 41–2; D.R. Brothwell, *Digging up Bones* (1981), pp. 163–4, 166.

40 Society of Antiquaries, *Ordinances and Regulations*, p. 103; *Ménagier de Paris*, p. 240; *Records of the Wardrobe and Household, 1286–1287* HMSO (1977), p. xxxiv; Thomas Austin, *Two Fifteenth Century Cookery Books* (1888), p. 28. For further royal fruit purchases by Edward I, see also *Liber Quotidianus Contrarotulatoris Garderobae*, (1787), p. 74.

41 Hieatt and Butler, *Curye on Inglysch*, p. 20; A.R. Myers, *The Household of Edward IV* (1959), p. 123. See Trevor Scully, *Chiquart's 'On Cookery'*, *A Fifteenth Century Savoyard Culinary Treatise* (1986), pp. xviii–xxv for a useful discussion on medieval dietary theory and practice.

42 Dyer, *Social Relations*, p. 196; Susan Kybett, 'Henry VIII: a Malnourished King', *History Today*, 39 (1989), pp. 19–25; Power, *Goodman of Paris*, pp. 238, 240; Salzman, *English Trade*, p. 413; Drummond and Wilbraham, *Englishman's Food*, pp. 68–9; *Records of the Wardrobe and Household 1285–1286*, pp. xxx, xxxiv, 585, 666; *Records of the Wardrobe and Household 1286–1289* (1986), pp. xvi, 384; Luisa Arano, *The Medieval Health Handbook, Tacuinum Sanitatis* (1976), illustrations; Michael Scott, *The Science of Dining (Mensa Philosophica)* (1936), p. 34. For the references to diets to prevent catching the plague, Karl Sudhoff, *Archiv fur Geschicte der Medizin*, Vol. 5 (1912), pp. 62–9 and Bengt Knuttson, *A Little Book for the Pestilence* (1911), I owe thanks to Dr Rosemary Horrox. They will appear in her forthcoming book on the Black Death. John Lydgate in his poem, 'A doctrine for the Pestilence', recommends the avoidance of fruit: Henry MacCracken (ed.), *Minor Poems*, Part II: *Secular Poems* (1934), p. 702.

43 For evidence of a mixed protein and vegetable diet eaten by medieval peasants, see G. Huhne-Osterloh and G. Grupe, 'Causes of Infant Mortality in the Middle Ages Revealed by Chemical and Palaeological Analyses of Skeletal Remains', *Zeitschrift fur Morphologia und Anthropologie*, 77 (1989), p. 251, (there is evidence that, in Schleswig in the twelfth century, the children of these peasants suffered from vitamin C deficiency, but this was probably due to bad weaning practices rather than a generally poor diet, p. 256). I owe thanks to W.J. White for this reference and for useful discussions on paleopathology in general. For a sauce containing all of these herbs, and more, see Hieatt and Butler, *Curye on Inglysch*, p. 130 Concerning the cooking time given to vegetables, it is said in Drummond and Wilbraham, *Englishman's Food*, p. 77, that there is evidence that some green vegetables at least were shredded and cooked quickly in butter or milk, which would tend to preserve the vitamin C.

44 'Cabbages and Chemistry', *New Scientist*, 131 (1779), p. 21; M. Wolfsperger, Dietary Habits of Historical Human Populations', *Ernaehrung (Vienna)*, Vol. 14 (1990), pp. 672–75; James Greig, 'The Investigation of a Medieval Barrel-latrine from Worcester', *Journal of Archaeological Science*, 8, p. 271 (this latrine was in the centre of Worcester); David Austin, 'Barnard Castle, Co. Durham Second Interim Report', *Journal of the British Archaeological Association*, 133, p. 87; Dyer, *Social Relations*, pp. 195, 196; Emmison, *Tudor Secretary*, p. 140; Mennell, *All Manners of Food*, p. 46; *Historical Manuscripts Commission, Sixth Report* (1871), Appx, p. 556.

45 J.M. Thurgood, 'The Diet and Domestic Households of the English Lay Nobility, 1265–1531', M Phil thesis, London University (1982), p. 202.

CHAPTER SIX: TABLE MANNERS

1 Hanawalt, *Ties That Bound*, pp. 60–1; Hilton, *Medieval Society*, pp. 104, 105; Miller and Hatcher, *Medieval England*, p. 158; Bennett, *English Manor*, pp. 232, 233.

2 F.J. Furnivall (ed.), *The Babees Book, the Boke of Nurture etc.* (1868), p.1; Myers, *Household of Edward*, p. 127.

3 Langland, *Piers the Plowman*, Vol. 1, p. 207, Vol. 2, p. 112; Borde, *Dyetary of Helth*, p. 251; Myers, *Household of Edward*, p. 213; Bridget Henisch, *Fast and Feast, Food in Medieval Society* (1976), pp. 20–1, 22–3.

4 Percy, *Northumberland Household*, pp. 65, 298, 305, 307; Henisch, *Fast and Feast*, pp. 17–18; John Lydgate, 'A dietary', *Minor Poems*, Vol. 2 (1934), p. 703; Nicholas Orme, 'The Education of Edward V', *Bulletin of the Institute of Historical Research*, Vol. 57 (1984), pp. 127, 128; Society of Antiquaries, *Ordinances and Regulations*, p. 37*; Henisch, *Fast and Feast*, pp. 18–20, 24; Myers, *Household of Edward*, p. 216. Harrison, *Description of England*, pp. 162, 166, suggests that, in his time, noble and gentlefolk dined at 11.00 am and supped at 5.00 pm, merchants at 12.00 noon and 6.00 p.m., husbandmen at 12.00 noon and 7.00 p.m. or 8.00 p.m. and scholars at 10.00 p.m.

5 Furnivall, *Babees Book*, pp. 66, (from the 'Boke of Nurture or

Schole of Gode Maners' of 1554 by Hugh Rhodes of the Chapel of Henry VIII), 121, 129 (from John Russell, 'Boke of Nurture', probably of the first third of the fifteenth century. Russell, Usher of the Chamber and Marshal of the Hall to Humphrey Duke of Gloucester, give a fascinating account of how the butler, enjoined at about this point in the proceedings to tap the wine barrels with his gimlets, augers and spouts, can avoid stirring up the lees when tapping a barrel. The butler and pantler seem to have been interchangeable in the fifteenth century. The pantler originally laid and cut the bread, later he and the butler laid the table: Furnivall, *Babees Book*, p. 312; Gerard Brett, *Dinner is Served: a History of Dining in England* (1968), pp. 31–2. The final quotation comes from a description by Froissart of a royal banquet in Paris in 1389: Jean Froissart, *Chronicles* (1902), Vol. 5, p. 281.

6   Henisch, *Fast and Feast*, pp. 148, 151, 154; Furnivall, *Babees Book*, p. 129 (Russell 'Boke of Nurture'). A very similar description of laying the cloth is given in Wynkyn de Woorde, Furnivall, 'Boke of Kervyng' *Babees Book* (1513), p. 268. This in turn seems to derive from a manuscript of the mid-fifteenth century, see N.R. Ker, *Medieval Manuscripts in British Libraries* (1969), p. 309.

7   Warner, *Antiquitates Culinariae*, p. 99; Brett, *Dinner is Served*, p. 56; Society of Antiquities, *Ordinances and Regulations*, p. 119; Oschinsky, *Walter of Henley*, p. 407.

8   Furnivall, *Babees Book*, pp. 66, 120; Bennett, *English Manor*, p. 262; Wilson, *Food and Drink*, p. 56. For trenchers in the household of the Earl of Northumberland, see above p. 87.

9   Warner, *Antiquitates Culinariae*, pp. 100–1; Furnivall, *Babees Book*, p. 67; Power, *Goodman of Paris*, p. 239.

10 Furnivall, *Babees Book*, pp. 66, 130; N.H. Nicolas, (ed.), *Testamenta Vetusta* (1826), Vol. 1, pp. 111, 141; Francis Palgrave (ed.), *The Antient Kalendars and Inventories of the Treasury*, Vol. 3 (1836), pp. 136, 320 (for the nef of Richard II see also Joan Evans, *English Art 1307–1461* (1949), p. 85).

11 Bridbury, *Salt Trade*, pp. 1–21, 51–2, 57, 98–9, 109; Warner, *Antiquitates Culinariae*, p. 103.

12 Furnivall, *Babees Book*, pp. 66–7, 130–1, 138–9; Henisch, *Fast and Feast*, pp. 158–9.

13 Henisch, *Fast and Feast*, pp. 180–9; Brett, *Dinner is Served*, pp. 61–2.

14 Henisch, *Fast and Feast*, pp. 165–8, 180–9; Furnivall, *Babees Book*, pp. 139, 322–3. For the 'assay': Furnivall, *Babees Book*, pp. 196–7, 322, 324–5 and other references. Care was taken to smooth the surnape, as well as the table cloth, see above and 'Ceremonies and Services at Court in the time of Henry VII': Francis Grose and Thomas Astle (eds), *Antiquarian Repertory*, Vol. 1 (1807), p. 322. The washing of hands has been considered from the point of view of cleanliness by Georges Vigarello, *Concepts of Cleanliness* (1988), pp. 45–8. Vigarello argues that hygiene had no part at all in the reasons for washing the hands but that the ceremony was only a question of good manners. However, given such facts as the regulations that apprentices had to be given clean bedding and clothing, the sale of soap, and the existence of public bath-houses in large medieval towns (Thrupp, *Merchant Class*, pp. 138–9), his argument seems hard to accept, at least in the sense of hygiene as a desire for cleanliness over dirtiness. I owe thanks to Miss Kay Staniland for drawing my attention to Vigarello's work.

15 Warner, *Antiquitates Culinariae*, p. 103; Furnivall, *Babees Book*, pp. 137–8 (unlacing and myncing both mean carving, tene is to trouble), 140–6, 158, 265, 324 (this from the 'Boke of Curtasye' of about 1430). For grace: Furnivall, *Babees Book*, pp. 323, 368–9.

16 Furnivall, *Babees Book*, pp. 67, 139

17 Furnivall, *Babees Book*, pp. 68, 133, 166, 168; Henisch, *Fast and Feast*, pp. 77, 202; Warner, *Antiquitates Culinariae*, p. 103; Wilson, *Food and Drink*, pp. 224, 226–7; Hieatt and Butler, *Curye on Inglysch*, pp. 148–50, 173, 179, 207; Simon, *Wine Trade*, Vol. 1, p. 290, Vol. 2, pp. 252–3. Clarry should not be confused with claret which was also drunk. For wine and ale cups, see Brett, *Dinner is Served*, pp. 75–7.

18 Warner, *Antiquitates Culinariae*, pp. 102–3; Society of Antiquaries, *Ordinances and Regulations*, pp. 29–30; Turner, *Manners and Household Expenses*, p. xxviii.

19 Furnivall, *Babees Book*, pp. 7, 68, 138–9. The following paragraph is also drawn in large part from this book; Henisch, *Fast and Feast*, p. 152.

20 Furnivall, *Babees Book*, pp. 6–7 (the 'Babees Book' itself, of about 1475), 75–6, (Rhodes's book), 138 (Russell's book); 300 ('Boke of Curtasye'); Jean-Claude Schmitt, *La Raison des Gestes dans L'Occident Medieval* (1990), p. 197.

21 Furnivall, *Babees Book*, pp. 188–9 (Russell, 'Boke of Nurture'); Myers, *Black Book*, p. 214.

22 Furnivall, *Babees Book*, pp. 7, 14, 18, 20, 29, 76–81.

23 Furnivall, *Babees Book*, pp. 79–82, 301.

24 Myers, *Household of Edward*, pp. 95–6, 99–100, 103–4, 129–130; Crawford, *Duke of Norfolk*, Vol. II, pp. 468–70, 475; Society of Antiquaries, *Ordinances and Regulations*, p. 105; Hamon le Strange, 'A Roll of the Household Accounts of Sir Hamon le Strange of Hunstanton, Norfolk, 1347–1348', *Archaeologia*, 69, p. 112; Dyer, *Standards of Living*, pp. 50–1.

25 Percy, *Northumberland Household*, pp. 45, 151–2; C.D. Ross, 'The Household Accounts of Elizabeth Berkeley, Countess of Warwick, 1420–1', *Transactions of the Bristol and Gloucester Archaeological Society*, Vol. 70, pp. 84, 90–91.

26 Sutton and Hammond, *Coronation of Richard*, pp. 251–2.

27 For discussion of the organization of the household 'below stairs', see Mertes, *English Noble Households*, pp. 32–42. See also Appendix *c*, p. 218 for the size of different households between 1250 and 1600.

28 Mertes, *English Noble Household*, p. 19; Myers, *Black Book*, pp. 71–5, 226–8 and references throughout.

29 Scully, *Chiquart*, pp. 12–13, 14, 15–16; Labarge, *Baronial Household*, pp. 117–18; Lucy Toulmin Smith (ed.), *Expeditions to Prussia and the Holy Land made by Henry Earl of Derby* (1894), pp. 101–2 (for a list of kitchen equipment supplied for Henry's use); Webb, *Expenses of Swinfield*, pp. liii–liv (a list of kitchen equipment bought). Chapter 4, 'Fuels and Fireplaces' in Dorothy Hartley, *Food in England* (1985), pp. 29–56 contains some interesting observations on cooking under the conditions in the medieval kitchen.

Notes

CHAPTER SEVEN: FEASTS

1   Alison Hanham (ed.), *The Cely Letters, 1472–1488*, (1975),
    pp. 26–7. For other similar secular and religious feasts, see
    Hanisch, *Fast and Feast*, pp. 51–2.

2   Kay Staniland, 'The Nuptials of Alexander III of Scotland and
    Margaret Plantagenet', *Nottingham Medieval Studies*, Vol. 30
    (1986), pp. 20–45. This article gives a clear picture of what
    went into the preparations (of all kinds, not just food) on such
    occasions. Thanks are due to Miss Staniland for drawing my
    attention to her article.

3   Hieatt and Butler, *Curye on Inglysch*, pp. 1, 7. For an
    interesting outline of the plan for a large feast, see Scully,
    Chiquart, pp. 8–9.

4   Hieeatt and Butler, *Curye on Inglysch*, pp. 8–10; Furnivall, *Babees
    Book*, p. 149

5   Henisch, *Fast and Feast*, p. 101; Cosman, *Fabulous Feasts*, p. 39;
    Power, *Goodman of Paris*, p. 241.

6   Austin, *Cookery Books*, p. 15; Hieatt and Butler, *Curye on
    Inglysch*, p. 155, 208–9. It has been suggested that medieval
    people knew of the medicinal value of some spices and used
    them for this reason. This seems unlikely. See Tannahill, *Food
    in History*, p. 167.

7   Percy, *Northumberland Household*, pp. 103–8. Many other birds
    are named, practically anything which could be eaten; Austin,
    Cookery Books, pp. 58, 59.

8   Austin, *Cookery Books*, p. 103; see also Henisch, *Fast and Feast*,
    p. 120.

9   W.E. Mead, *The English Medieval Feast* (1967), p. 155;
    Furnivall, *Babees Book*, Part II, pp. 39, 41 for the *Modus
    Lenandi*; R.W. Chambers (ed.), *A Fifteenth Century Courtesy
    Book*, (1914), p. 17; Hieatt and Butler, *Curye on Inglysch*,
    pp. 3–5. The suggested pattern for a fast day seems to have
    been partly followed by Chiquart Amiezo, cook to Amadeus
    Count of Savoy, in 1403: Scully, *Chiquart*, pp. 117, 118.

10 Power, *Goodman of Paris*, pp. 238–9, 330; Brereton and Ferrier,
    Ménagier de Paris, p. 148.

11 Power, *Goodman of Paris*, p. 34; Brereton and Ferrier, *Ménagier de
    Paris*, p. 184.

12 Power, *Goodman of Paris*, p. 239; Brereton and Ferrier, *Ménagier de Paris*, pp. 184–5, 319.

13 Power, *Goodman of Paris*, pp. 241–2, 244; Brereton and Ferrier, *Ménagier de Paris*, p. 321.

14 Power, *Goodman of Paris*, pp. 242, 243, 244. The *portechappes* were members of the guild of cooks and provided the bread. They also seem to have hired out vessels and other necessities for feasts: Brereton and Ferrier, *Menagier de Paris*, p. 320.

15 Sutton and Hammond, *Coronation of Richard*, pp. 282, 294–5.

16 For a brief discussion of the number of dishes in other fourteenth- and fifteenth-century coronations, see Sutton and Hammond, *Coronation of Richard*, pp. 285–6. Very useful glossaries of cooking terms are found in Austin, *Cookery Books*; Hieatt and Butler, *Curye on Inglysch*, and Sutton and Hammond. For 'compost' see Hieatt and Butler, p. 13.

17 Sutton and Hammond, *Coronation of Richard*, p. 295.

18 Austin, *Cookery Books*, pp. 67, 79 (for roasting birds); Labarge, *Baronial Household*, p. 82.

19 Austin, *Cookery Books*, p. 19; Hieatt and Butler, *Curye on Inglysch*, pp. 8, 108.

20 Scully, *Chiquart*, p. 116. See OED under Dragon's blood and purple.

21 Mead, *Medieval Feast*, pp. 102–5 (for the multicoloured fish dish, see p. 105); Hieatt and Butler, *Curye on Inglysch*, p. 131.

22 Hieatt and Butler, *Curye on Inglysch*, pp. 139; Lydgate, *Minor Poems*, Vol. 2, p. 628; Scully, *Chiquart*, pp. 53, 117.

23 Austin, *Cookery Books*, p. 79.

24 Hieatt and Butler, *Curye on Inglysch*, p. 143; Power, *Goodman of Paris*, pp. 227, 239; John Russell, 'Boke of Nurture' in Furnivall, *Babees Book*, pp. 125–8 gives a detailed (if slightly confusing) description of how to make hippocras. Russell recommends using the spices again in the kitchen. Two other, less complicated recipes are given in Richard Arnold, *Chronicle* (1811), p. 187.

25 Hieatt and Butler, *Curye on Inglysch*, pp. 145, 148, 178–9; Henisch, *Fast and Feast*, p. 77; Power, *Goodman of Paris*, p. 226; Furnivall, *Babees Book*, pp. 122, 280.

26 Hieatt and Butler, *Curye on Inglysch*, pp. 2–4. Other menus can be found in Austin, *Cookery Books*, pp. 57–64, 67–9, in Furnivall,

Notes

Babees Book, pp. 164–8, and in Power, *Goodman of Paris*, pp. 226–36.

27 Furnivall, *Babees Book*, p. 166 for Russell's sample menus; Power, *Goodman of Paris*, p. 25; Hieatt and Butler, *Curye on Inglysch*, pp. 99, 115; Austin, *Cookery Books*, p. 69; Turner, *Manners and Expenses*, p. xlvii, (for Kymer himself, see p.xxxvii).

28 Henisch, *Fast and Feast*, pp. 108–11; Crawford, *Duke of Norfolk*, Vol. II, p. 398; Harrison, *Description of England*, p. 324.

29 Power, *Goodman of Paris*, p. 242.

30 Henisch, *Fast and Feast*, pp. 230–1; A.H. Thomas and I.D. Thornley (eds), *The Great Chronicle of London* (1938), pp. 117–19.

31 Lydgate, *Minor Poems*, pp. 623–4; John Leland, *De Rebus Britannicis Collectanea*, Vol. 4 (1774), p. 226.

32 Furnivall, *Babees Book*, pp. 164–9; Austin, *Cookery Books*, pp. 62–3, 69. The description of the subtelty from Archbishop Stafford's feast changes from English to Latin half way through.

33 Constance Bullock-Davies, *Menestrellorum Multitudo* (1978), pp. 11–12, 23–4; C.H. Cooper, *Annals of Cambridge*, Vol. 1, 1842, p. 230; Percy, *Northumberland Household*, p. 327.

34 Henisch, *Fast and Feast*, pp. 210–12; Glynne Wickham, *Early English Stages 1300–1576* (1959) pp. 17–18.

35 Bullock-Davies, *Menestrellorum Multitudo*, pp. 26, 55–60; Henisch, *Fast and Feast*, p. 208.

36 Bullock-Davies, *Menestrellorum Multitudo*, pp. 16–17, 19, 25–6, 159–62 (for 'King Robert'). For a most interesting discussion of medieval musical instruments in 1306, see pp. 27–38; Percy, *Northumberland Household*, p. 331; Society of Antiquaries, *Ordinances and Regulations*, pp. 4, 11; Myers, *Household of Edward*, pp. 131–2, Sutton and Hammond, *Coronation of Richard*, p. 78–9.

37 Mead, *Medieval Feast*, pp. 173–4; Henisch, *Fast and Feast*, p. 217.

38 Henisch, *Fast and Feast*, pp. 220–9; Wickham, *English Stages*, pp. 17–18, 191–5. For dating Lydgate's 'mummings', see Walter Schirmer, *John Lydgate: a Study in the Culture of the Fifteenth Century* (1961), p. 106.

39 Wickham, *English Stages*, pp. 210–11; Cosman, *Fabulous Feasts*, pp. 31, 32; Anthony R. Wagner, 'The Swan Badge and the Swan Knight', *Archaeologia*, 97 (1959), p. 132.

40 Bullock-Davies, *Menestrellorum Multitudo*, pp. xxix–xxxvi. For

reference to the use of the swan, see Wagner, *Archaeologia*, Vol. 97, (1959).

41 Henisch, *Fast and Feast*, pp. 198–9; Froissart, *Chronicles*, Vol. 5, p. 282; Wickham, *English Stages*, pp. 212–7. Mummings, disguising and 'interludes' are discussed thoroughly by Wickham; Scully, *Chiquart*, pp. 30–6.

42 Gordon Kipling (ed.), *The Receyt of the Ladie Katheryne* (1990), pp. xx, 55–6, 66.

AFTERWORD

1   White, pp. 81, 82, 83
2   White, pp. 36–41
3   Woolgar, pp. 111, 112
4   Woolgar, pp. 111, 113, 132
5   White, pp. 77–8
6   Scully, Art, pp. 42–4, 186 et seq.
7   Brears, pp. 117–18
8   Scully, Art, pp. 87–9, 93–9
9   Scully, Art, pp. 8, 24–5
10 Woolgar, p. 84
11 Woolgar, table, p. 85; Scully, Art, pp. 119–20
12 Worde, p. 7, diagram, p. 75
13 Worde, pp. 80–3

BIBLIOGRAPHY

Amherst, Alicia. 'A Fifteenth Century Treatise on Gardening by Mayster Ion Gardener', *Archaeologia*, 54. 1894.

Arano, Luisa. *The Medieval Health Handbook, Tacuinum Sanitatis*. 1986.

Archer, Ian, Barron, Caroline and Harding, Vanessa. *Hugh Alley's Caveat: The Markets of London in 1598*, London, London Topographical Society. 1988.

Ashley, W. *The Bread of Our Forefathers*. 1928.

Austin, T. *Two Fifteenth Century Cookery Books*. Early English Text Society, 1888.

Bennett, H.S. *Life on the English Manor*. 1937.

Bennett, Judith. 'Conviviality and Charity in Medieval and Early Modern England', *Past and Present*, 134. 1992.

Bolton, J.L. *The Medieval English Economy 1150–1500*. 1985.

Bond, C.J. 'Monastic Fisheries' in *Medieval Fish, Fisheries and Fishponds in England*, Michael Aston (ed.), 1988.

Borde, Andrew. *A Compendyous Regyment or a Dietary of Helth*, F.J. Furnivall (ed.) Early English Text Society, 1907.

Brears, Peter, *All the Kings Cooks, The Tudor Kitchens of King Henry VIII at Hampton Court*, 1999

Brereton, Georgine and Ferrier, Janet. *Le Ménagier de Paris*. 1981.

Brett, Gerard. *Dinner is Served: A History of Dining in England 1400–1900*. 1968.

Bridbury, Anthony. *England and the Salt Trade in the Later Middle Ages*. 1955.

Brothwell, D.R. *Digging Up Bones*. 1981.

Bullock-Davies, Constance. *Menestrellorum Multitudo*. 1978.

Calendar of Liberate Rolls 1245–1251. London, HMSO, 1937.

Calendar of Liberate Rolls 1260–1267. London, HMSO, 1961.

Calendar of Patent Rolls, Henry VI, 1441–1446. 1908.

Carus-Wilson, E.M. *Overseas Trade of Bristol in the Later Middle Ages*. 1937.

Cely Letters, Alison Hanham (ed.). Early English Text Society, 1975.

Chambers, R.A. and Gray, M. 'The Excavation of Fishponds' in *Medieval Fish, Fisheries and Fishponds in England*, Michael Aston (ed.). 1988.

Chambers, R.W. *A Fifteenth Century Courtesy Book*. Early English Text Society, 1914.

Chaney, Margaret and Ross, Margaret. *Nutrition*. 1971.

Chaucer, Geoffrey. *Complete Works*. Walter Skeat (ed.), Vol. 4. 1896.

Clarke, P. *The English Alehouse: a Social History 1200–1830*. 1983.

Clay, Rotha. *Medieval Hospitals of England*. 1909.

Cobb, H.S. *Overseas Trade of London: Exchequer Customs Accounts 1480–81*. London, London Record Society, 1990.

Collection of Ordinances and Regulations for the Royal Household. Society of Antiquaries, 1790.

Connor, R.D. *Weights and Measures of England*. 1987.

Cooper, C.H. *Annals of Cambridge*, Vol. 1. 1842.

Cosman, Madeleine. *Fabulous Feasts: Medieval Cookery and Ceremony*. 1976.

Crawford, Anne. *The Household Books of John Howard, Duke of Norfolk, 1462–1471, 1481–1483*. 1992.

Cust, Mrs Henry. *Gentlemen Errant*. 1909.

Dale, M.K. and Redstone, V.B. *The Household Book of Dame Alice de Bryene of Acton Hall, Suffolk, September 1412–September 1413*. Suffolk Institute of Archaeology, 1931.

Davenport, F.G. *The Economic Development of a Norfolk Manor, 1086–1565*. 1906.

Davies, C.S.L. 'Les rations alimentaires de l'armée et de la marine anglaises au XVIth siècle', in *Pour une histoire de l'alimentation: Cahiers des Annales, 28*. 1970.

Dobson, R.B. *Durham Priory 1400–1450*. 1973.

Drummond, J.C. and Wilbraham, Anne. *The Englishman's Food*. 1958.

Duby, Georges. *Rural Economy and Rural Life in the Medieval West*. 1968.

Bibliography

Dyer, Christopher. 'English Diet in the Later Middle Ages', in *Social Relations and Ideas*, T.H. Aston *et al.*, (eds). 1983.

Dyer, Christopher. *Standards of Living in the Middle Ages*. 1989.

Emmison, F.G. *Tudor Secretary, Sir William Petre at Court and Home*. 1961.

Ernle, Lord. *English Farming Past and Present*. 1936.

Farley, J.S. *City Government of Winchester*. 1923.

Farley, J.S. *Town Life in the Fourteenth Century as seen in the Court Rolls of Winchester City*. 1942.

Filby, F.A. *A History of Food Adulteration and Analysis*. 1934.

Furnivall, F.J. (ed.). *Babees Book, the Boke of Nurture etc.*, Early English Text Society, 1868.

Galloway, James and Murphy, Margaret. 'Feeding the City, Medieval London and its Hinterland', *The London Journal*, 16. 1991.

Given-Wilson, Chris. *The English Nobility in the Middle Ages*. 1987.

Graham, Helena. 'A Womans Work . . .': Labour and Gender in the Late Medieval Countryside', in *Woman is a Worthy Wight: Women in English Society, c.1200–1500*, P.J.P. Goldberg (ed.). 1992.

Green, Mrs J.R. *Town Life in the Fifteenth Century*. 1894.

Greig, James. 'The Investigation of a Medieval Barrel-Latrine from Worcester', *Journal of Archaeological Science*, 8. 1981.

Grose, Francis. *The Antiquarian Repertory*, Vol. 1. 1807.

Hall, Hubert. *Society in the Elizabethan Age*. 1902.

Hammond, Eleanor. 'London Lickpenny', *Anglia*, Vol. 20. 1898.

Hanawalt, B. *The Ties that Bound: Peasant Families in Medieval England*. 1986.

Harris, Mary. *Coventry Leet Book*, Part III. Early English Text Society, 1909.

Harris, Mary. *The Account of the Great Household of Humphrey First Duke of Buckingham, for the Year 1452–53*, Camden Miscellany Vol. xxviii, 1984.

Harrison, William. *Description of England*, F.J. Furnivall (ed.). 1877.

Hartley, Dorothy. *Food in England*. 1985.

Harvey, P.D.A. *A Medieval Oxfordshire Village: Cuxham 1240–1400*. 1962.

Henisch, Bridget. *Fast and Feast, Food in Medieval Society*. 1976.

Hieatt, Constance and Butler, Sharon. *Curye on Inglysch: English Culinary Manuscripts of the Fourteenth Century*, Early English Text Society, 1985.

Hilton, R.H. *A Medieval Society: the West Midlands at the End of the Thirteenth Century.* 1966.

Homans, G.C. *English Villagers of the Thirteenth Century.* 1942.

Hone, Nathaniel. *The Manor and Manorial Records.* 1906.

Innes, C. *Ledger of Andrew Halyburton.* 1867.

James, Margery. *Studies in the Medieval Wine Trade.* Elspeth Veale (ed.). 1971.

Jones, P.E. *Butchers of London.* 1976.

Keen, Maurice. *English Society in the Later Middle Ages 1348–1500.* 1990.

Keene, Derek. 'Shops and Shopping in Medieval London', *Medieval Art, Architecture and Archaeology in London*, Lindy Grant (ed.). 1990.

Kershaw, Ian. *Bolton Priory.* 1973.

Kipling, Gordon. *The Receyt of the Ladie Katheryne.* Early English Text Society, 1990.

Kitchin, G.W. *Compotus Rolls of the Obedientaries of St Swithuns Priory, Winchester,* 1892.

Kybett, Susan. 'Henry VIII, a malnourished King', *History Today*, 39, 1989.

Labarge, Margaret Wade. *A Baronial Household of the Thirteenth Century.* 1965.

Lane, Frederic. 'Salaires et régimes alimentaires des marins vénitiens au début du xivth siècle', in *Pour une histoire de l'alimentation*: *Cahiers des Annales*, 28, (1970).

Langland, William. *The Vision of William Concerning Piers the Plowman.* Walter Skeat (ed.). 1886.

Le Strange, Hamon. 'A Roll of the Household Accounts of Sir Hamon le Strange of Hunstanton, Norfolk, 1347–1348', *Archaeologia*, 69, 1920.

Leland, John. *De Rebus Britannicis Collectanea*, Vol. 4. 1774.

Liber Quotidianus Contrarotulatoris Garderobae. Society of Antiquaries, 1787.

Livi-Bacci, Massimo. *Population and Nutrition: an Essay on European Demographic History.* Cambridge, Cambridge University Press, 1991.

Lumiansky, R.M. and David Mills. *The Chester Mystery Cycle*, Early English Text Society, 1974.

Lydgate, John. *The Minor Poems. Part II: Secular Poems*, Henry MacCracken (ed.). Early English Text Society, 1934.

Bibliography

McIntosh, Marjorie. *Autonomy and Community: the Royal Manor of Havering, 1200–1500*. 1986.

McIntosh, Marjorie. *A Community Transformed: The Manor and Liberty of Havering, 1500–1620*. 1991.

McLean, Teresa. *Medieval English Gardens*. 1981.

Mead, W.E. *The English Medieval Feast*. 1967.

Mennell, Stephen. *All Manners of Food*. 1985.

Mertes, Kate. *The English Noble Household, 1250–1600*. 1988.

Miller, Edward and Hatcher, John. *Medieval England: Rural Society and Economic Change*. 1978.

Monckton, H.A. *A History of English Ale and Beer*. 1966.

Moorhouse, S. 'Medieval Fishponds: Some Thoughts', in *Medieval Fish, Fisheries and Fishponds in England*, Michael Aston (ed.). 1988.

Myer, A.R. *The Household of Edward IV*. 1958.

Nicolas, N.H. *Testamenta Vetusta*. 1826.

Ordish, S. *Wine Growing in England*. 1953.

Orme, Nicholas. 'The Education of Edward V', *Bulletin of the Institute of Historical Research*, 57, 1984.

Oschinsky, Dorothea. *Walter of Henley and other Treatises on Estate Management and Accounting*. 1971.

Palladius on Husbandry. Early English Text Society. 1873/1879.

Palliser, D.M., *Tudor York*. 1965.

Paul, A.A. and Southgate, D.A.T., *McCance and Widdowson's The Composition of Foods*. 1978.

Percy, Thomas. *The Regulations and the Household of Henry Algernon Percy the Fifth Earl of Northumberland*. 1905.

Power, Eileen and Postan, M.M. *Studies in English Trade in the Fifteenth Century*. 1933.

Power, Eileen (ed., trs.). *The Goodman of Paris*. 1928.

Prestwich, Michael. 'Victualling Estimates for English Garrisons in Scotland during the Fourteenth Century', *English Historical Review*, 82, 1967.

Pullein, C. *Rotherfield*. Tunbridge Wells, 1928.

Records of the Wardrobe and Household, 1286–1289. London, HMSO, 1986.

Records of the Wardrobe and Household, 1285–1286. London, HMSO, 1977.

Richmond, Colin. *John Hopton, A Fifteenth Century Suffolk Gentleman*. 1981.

Riley, Henry. *Memorials of London and London Life*. 1878.

Riley, H.T. (ed.). *Munimenta Gildhallae Londoniensis: Liber Albus, Liber Custumarum et Liber Horn*, Rolls Series, (1849–62).

Rogers, J.E. Thorold. *A History of Agriculture and Prices in England*, Vol. 1, 1866.

Rogers, J.E. Thorold. *A History of Agriculture and Prices in England*. Vol. 4. 1866.

Ross, C.D. 'The Household Accounts of Elizabeth Berkeley, Countess of Warwick, 1420–1', *Transactions of the Bristol and Gloucester Archaeological Society*. vol. 70, 1951.

Rosser, Gervase. *Medieval Westminster, 1200–1540*. 1989.

Salusbury, G.T. *Street Life in Medieval England*. 1948.

Salzman, L.F. *English Life in the Middle Ages*. 1927.

Salzman, L.F. *English Trade in the Middle Ages*. 1931.

Saul, A. 'The Herring Industry in Great Yarmouth', *Norfolk Archaeology* 38, 1983.

Schirmer, Walter. *John Lydgate: a Study in the Culture of the Fifteenth Century*. 1961.

Schmitt, Jean-Claude. *La Raison des Gestes dans l'Occident Médiéval*. 1990.

Scott, Michael. *The Science of Dining*, Arthur Way (trs.). 1936.

Scully, Terence. *Chiquart's 'On Cookery': A Fifteenth Century Savoyard Culinary Treatise*. 1986.

Scully, *The Art of Cookery in the Middle Ages*, 2000

Scully, *The Vivendier: A Fifteenth Century French Cookery Manuscript*, 1997

Secretum Secretorum, M.A. Manzalaoui (ed.). Early English Text Society, 1977.

Sharpe, Reginald. *Calendar of the Letter Books of the City of London: Letter Books A–K*. 1900–1912.

Simon, Andre. *The History of the Wine Trade in England*. 1906.

Skeat, Walter. *Pierce the Ploughman's Crede*. Early English Text Society, 1867.

Staniland, Kay. 'The Nuptials of Alexander III of Scotland and Margaret Plantagenet', *Nottingham Medieval Studies*, vol. 30, 1986.

Steane, J.M. 'The Royal Fishponds of Medieval England', in *Medieval Fish, Fisheries and Fishponds in England*, Michael Aston (ed.). 1988.

Bibliography

Stow, John. *A Survey of London*, C.L. Kingsford (ed.). 1908.

Sutton, Anne and Hammond, P.W. *The Coronation of Richard III*. 1983.

Swanson, Heather. *Medieval Artisans: An Urban Class in Late Medieval England*. 1989.

Tannahill, Reay. *Food in History*. 1988.

Taylor, C.C. 'Problems and Possibilities', in *Medieval Fish, Fisheries and Fishponds in England*, Michael Aston (ed.). 1988.

Thomas, A.H. and Thornley, I.D. *The Great Chronicle of London*. 1938.

Thrupp, S.J. *The Merchant Class of Medieval London*. 1948.

Thurgood, J.M. 'The Diet and Domestic Households of the English Lay Nobility, 1265–1531', M.Phil thesis, London University, 1982.

Truswell, A. Stewart. *ABC of Nutrition*. 1986.

Turner, T.H. *Manners and Household Expenses of England in the Thirteenth and Fifteenth Centuries*. 1841.

Wagner, Anthony. 'The Swan Badge and the Swan Knight', *Archaeologia*, 97, 1959.

Warner, Richard. *Antiquitates Culinariae*. 1791.

Webb, John. *Roll of the Household Expenses of Richard de Swinfield, Bishop of Hereford during the Years 1289 and 1290*. Camden Society, 1854 and 1855.

Wheaton, Barbara. *Savouring the Past* (1983), pp. 17–18.

White, W.J. *Skeletal Remains from the Cemetery of St Nicholas Shambles, City of London*. London and Middlesex Archaeological Society. 1988.

White, Eileen, (ed), *Feeding a City: York*, 2000

Wickham, Glynne. *Early English Stages 1300–1576*. 1959.

Wilson, C. Anne. *Food and Drink in Britain*. 1984.

Wolfsperger, M. 'Dietary Habits of Historical Human Populations, *Ernaehrung*, Vienna, 14. 1990.

Wood-Legh, K.L. *A Small Household of the XVth Century*. 1956.

Woolgar, C M, *The Great Household in Late Medieval England*, 1999

Worde, Wynkyn de, *Boke of Keruynge*, (with an Introduction by Peter Brears), 2003

INDEX

Index

basil, 41
baskets, 123
bass, 44
bastard wine, 55
Bath and Wells, Bishop of, 73
Bay salt, 109
beans, 2, 3, 40, 138, in peasant diet, 26, 28, 30, 31
Beaulieu Abbey, Hampshire, 20
Beauvais, Bishop of, 130
beaver tail, 69
Beckington, Bishop, 54
beef cattle, 73
beef, 58, 62, 69, 71, broth, 127, price, 82, ribs, 49
beer, 6, 72, acceptance of, antagonism to, 82–3, components, 83, double-double, 52, introduction, 82, price, 82, strength, 52,
Beerbrewers, Guild, 83
beet, 40
behaviour, at mealtimes, 115, 117
berevechicorn, 3
Berkeley, Countess of, size of household, 119, Lord, 10, Maurice, fourth lord, 36, Sir Thomas, 74
Berkeley, Gloucestershire, 74
Berwick on Tweed, 20
Bicester Priory, Oxfordshire, 19
bilberries, 100
biotin, 107
birds, catching, 16, exotic, 127, small, 127, 128
birlesters, 44
bis, 45
Bishopstone, Suffolk, 33
bittern, 133, cooked, price, 47
Black Death, fruit diet, 99
blankmanger, 131
blaunchpoudre, 65
blaundsorr, 134
blood, as food colour, 135
boar, 18, 60, 64, for feast, 125
Boar's Head tavern, Westminster, 49
Boke of Curtasye, 110
Boke of Nurture, 127, 140
bollymong (bullymong), 3

Bolton Priory, Yorkshire, 26, 32, 73
boon work, 32, 33, 69, 70
borage, 41
Borde, Andrew, 83, 87–8, 104
Bourgneuf, Bay of, 109
bowls, wooden, 102
Boxley Abbey, Kent, 20
bramble fruits, 100
bran, 67, in diet, 95
braun, 18
bread, 26–7, 28, 62, 73, adulterated, 77, assise of bread, 41, 46, 51, 75, barley, 28, bean, 27, bis, 45, 'black', 66, bran in, 95, cocket, 45, feast, 125, fibre in, 95 harvest loaves, 69, importance of, 45, light weight, 77, manchet, 45, 72, 109, maslin, 72, paindemaigne, 45, quality, 76, regulations for sale, 45, rye, 27, 28, 33, 46, servants, 73, tourte, 45, trencher, 70, 72, 107, trete, 45, varieties, 45, wastel, 45, wheat, 32, white, 45, 109
Bread Street, London, 47, 50
breakfast, 105
bream, 23, 71
brewers, small scale, 49, women, 6, 49, 81–2
Brewers Company, London, 83
brewing, 6–7
Bridport, Dorset, 58
Bristol, port, 1, 2, 21
Bromhead Priory, Norfolk, 20
broth, 30
Broughton, Cambs, 33
Bruce, Robert, 145
bruet, (brewet) 134
Bryene, Dame Alice de, 61, 63, 68, 70, 92, 104, size of household, 118, wine bought, 68
Buckingham, Henry Stafford, Duke of, 6, 65, ale brewed in large amounts, 71
bucks, 71
Bude, Cornwall, 20
Burgundy, John, Duke of, 136, Philip the Good, Duke of, 144
Burgundy, wine, 13

Index

Index

Index